INTERNATIONAL   W9-AYY-628

EDITED BY EDMUND R. BROWN

THE MAKROPOULOS SECRET

Other Titles From:

INTERNATIONAL : POCKET : LIBRARY

THE
MAKROPOULOS SECRET

By KAREL CAPEK
Author of R. U. R.

Adapted by Randal C. Burrell
Introduction by H. T. Parker

BOSTON
INTERNATIONAL POCKET LIBRARY

PRINTED IN THE UNITED STATES OF AMERICA
BY THE COLONIAL PRESS INC., CLINTON, MASS.

INTRODUCTION

THE Makropoulos Secret was first played in the National Theater of Prague in November of 1922, and it was then that Karel Capek wrote to his audience:

"The idea of this new comedy first occurred to me about three or four years ago, before writing 'R. U. R.' It seemed then to be an ideal subject for a novel, but that is a form of writing I do not care for. The idea itself came from the theory of Professor Mecnik, that age is caused by an auto-intoxicating organism.

"I make these statements because Bernard Shaw's new play, 'Back to Methuselah,' which I have seen in synopsis only, appeared this winter. In actual measure, it is very impressive. It, too, has the motif of longevity. This likeness in theme is entirely accidental, and, it seems to me from the synopsis, that while Bernard Shaw comes to the same conclusion as I do, it is in quite the opposite manner. Mr. Shaw believes that it is possible for an ideal community of people to live several hundred years in a sort of paradise. As the play-goer perceives, long life in my play is treated quite differently; I think that such a condition is neither ideal nor desirable. Both ideas are purely hypothetical since neither has the proof of experience. Yet perhaps I may say this much: Mr. Shaw's play is a classic example of optimism, and my own — a hopeless instance of pessimism.

"Whether I am called an optimist or a pessimist, will make me neither happier nor sadder; yet, 'to be a pessimist' implies, it would seem, a silent rebuke from the world for bad behavior. In this comedy I have striven to present something delightful and optimistic. Does the optimist believe that it is bad to live sixty years but good to live three hundred? I merely think that when I proclaim a life of the ordinary span of sixty years as good enough in this world, I am not guilty of criminal pessimism. If we

5

say that, at some future time, there will be no disease, misery, or poverty—that certainly is optimism. If we say that this daily life of ours, full of deprivation and sorrow, is not really so irreconcilable, but has in it something of immense value—is that pessimism? I think not. One turns from bad to higher things: the other searches for something better and higher in ordinary existence. The one looks for paradise—there is not a loftier vision for the human soul—the other strives for recompense in life itself. Is this pessimism?"

In that Europe which is old and wise and patient and exacting, a man does not set to a task in the arts until he has learned how to use his medium and his tools. Therefore is Karel Capek expert craftsman of the theater. Two years and a half ago, Americans were discovering him in "R. U. R." as produced in New York by the Theater Guild, and great was their joy of him. Soon they knew him and his brother both in "The Insect Comedy," and substantial and stimulating were the satisfactions. By that time "The Makropoulos Secret" had been acted in Budapest, and producing managers in America were making speed to scan a rough draft of the play. Perhaps the managers failed to visualize it in actual representation—an outlook sometimes denied them. Possibly, like good Americans, they believed that all things go in spasms and that "the Capek boom" in our theater was nearly past. More singularly, none of our leading actresses seems to have known or sought the piece. Yet for them it contains the high-pitched, the all-pervading, the virtuosa part of a generation.

The technician and the layman sit alike in admiration before a playwright who can arrest attention and kindle interest in the very first speeches of his play; who can coördinate the introduction of the personages into the progress of the narrative; who from the interaction of both can quicken premises into curiosity aroused and suspense set a-vibrating. Of such a Capek is the first act of "The Makropoulos Secret." Before it is done we are engrossed in the suit of Gregor against Prus—a hundred years ago; in Emilia Marty, singing-woman, mysterious intervener and informer; in the spell she lays with nearly every contact; in the fulfilment forthwith of her sayings. Prus, Gregor, Vitek, Kolonaty have all come, as well, into individual human and theatric being.

A second act that apparently begins in decoration, only deepens the mystery and intensifies the fascination hanging about Elina-Emilia. Incidents that pass as the embroidery, almost the digression of the moment—say the interchanges between the young lovers—speedily contribute to the main course of the dramatic narrative, the rising current of dramatic suspense. For the while, Capek seems to be taking the permissible privilege of the playwright to amusing conversation—and lo! almost every sentence is contributing to the riddle of Emilia. Quick, hard, terse and tense come the two strokes at the end. At the blow and aim unmissed, the playwright hammers home.

"The toils are laid, the stakes are set." A third act ensues—of the steeled Emilia caught in a press that may crush even steel; of Emilia spent, desperate, menaced, disclosing at last the mystery that has haunted the play. Again there are interludes—Prus's discovery of the suicide of his son because the father had won the woman that the youth also craved; the foolish interventions of old Hauk-Sendorf. Yet the one is as the red bolt to pierce these darkening clouds; the other as the irony attending nearly every human crisis. "The melodrama, the staginess, the superfluity of the mock mediæval inquisition!" the reader is quick to say, as he cons the manuscript. Capek, however, writes for the stage, not for the easy-chair. In the theater these trappings retort with spell against spell upon the wavering Emilia. Nay, with them as well as with his hands, the justiciar clutches her by the throat and bids her exude the secret.

The woman reveals it and the suspense of the play seems ended—only to renew itself. For what shall be done with life everlasting? And in the next room Elena-Emilia waits. There is debate, in which the debaters speak also in character and with emotion. There is human decision. For Elena-Emilia there is also human release. So does the masterful Capek, abounding round a play that emotionally and suspensively seemed already full-circled.

Such work of the theater stirs the pride, quickens the zest of those who still love it, unashamed and unflagging, as seat—from time to time—of the arts. Yet Capek and "The Makropoulos Secret" would not so prevail unless they carried freight of matter to engage the mind, quicken the imagination, stir the spirit—matter, moreover, intrinsically human in content and implication, by the playwright and the stage vitalized. "The Makropoulos Secret" is the secret of life unending. The mystery of Emilia Marty, born Elena Makropoulos, is the mystery of endless existence dovetailing into the daily lives of men and women that are mortal. Her spell is the spell of a woman persisting and all-knowing, case-hardened in the virtue and vice, the experience and the sensation, of a life that has ceased to begin and wax, to waver and decline—a life that is perpetual. The secret once disclosed, the mystery once dispelled, it is as though a flood of light were bathing every facet of Elena-Emilia, pouring into every devious nook and dark corner of her courses before and within the play; beating upon every reaction in those about her.

Matter of fantasy, it is true, but matter that weaves these imaginings into the actualities of human experience. Matter of the theater, it is also true, but matter impregnated with human content and choice, speculation and even philosophy. Matter indeed of substance and vitality for the mind, the imagination and the spirit. And it is these things that Capek sums in the epilogue of debate and decision. For the while Emilia has quit the scene. The lawyer, the clerk, the nobleman, the suitor, youth in the girl, Kristina, senility in doddering Sendorf, hold in their hands the formula of everlasting life. With it they might lengthen, ripen and fill to brimming human days; breed an aristocracy of supermen; alter the whole course and custom of terrestrial existence. Emilia, who was Elena, slips through the door. From mind and heart upon her lips is the tale, the burden, the penalty of this life everlasting, wherein all sensations, emotions, impulses, experiences, numb into an eternal monotony of repetition. She is as mirror to the woman unperturbed by the suicide of the boy, undismayed when the trap closes upon her.

Bearing testimony, Elena-Emilia gives also verdict. Youth in Kristina; age in Sendorf; perception, understanding, sympathy and release in the others—affirm it. In the candle, the formula burns to ashes. From the window those ashes are scattered to the winds. Humanity as well as Elena Makropoulos is released from the eternities, rebound in the mortalities. It has its will; it is content, though the ironies try to laugh upon the woman's lips. "And what deterred you," the others have asked her, "from finding your own means of escape?" She answers: "I was afraid of death." In Sæcula Sæculorum.

H. T. PARKER

CAST OF CHARACTERS

EMILIA MARTY
JAROSLAV PRUS
ALBERT GREGOR
JANEK PRUS
KRISTINA
DR. KOLONATY
HAUK-SENDORF
VITEK
MECHANIC
SCRUBWOMAN
EMILIA'S MAID
PHYSICIAN

Act I.   *Dr. Kolonaty's law office*
Act II.   *The stage of a theater*
Act III. *Emilia Marty's boudoir at an hotel*

THE MAKROPOULOS SECRET

ACT I

(*The outer office of Dr. Kolonaty, Attorney at Law in a provincial city of the old Austro-Hungarian empire.*

The musty furniture, the accumulation of books and papers and, in particular, the tall document file at the back of the room, whose many pigeonholes are stuffed with the briefs of long-forgotten cases, plainly show that Dr. Kolonaty's is a comfortably established practice which has passed through several generations of the same family. In the rear is a door opening from the outer hallway and, on the left, is another door leading presumably to the inner offices. The clerk, Vitek, whom Dr. Kolonaty inherited along with the furniture and the clientele, has a small, flat-topped desk at the left. On it is a confused mass of maps, proclamations, law briefs; and a telephone. In the center of the room is a double desk and, on the right are several chairs.

At the rise of the curtain Vitek is seated on the top of a step-ladder, beside the file. His hands are full of these ancient papers which he is busily rearranging. At last they are all put away except one large group, tied together. He pauses in his work and turns round.)

VITEK.   Gregor vs. Prus.—The case of Gregor vs. Prus —you're finished. (*He sighs.*) Ah, well. (*Thumbing the briefs*) Eighteen twenty-seven—eighteen thirty-two—thirty-two—eighteen forty—forty—forty—forty-seven—and so on. Why, in three years we could have had a centennial jubilee! Finished. Such a good case, too! (*He pushes them into one of the pigeonholes.*) Here lies Gregor vs. Prus. Oh, nothing lives forever—*vanitas*. Dust and ashes! Baron Prus—the old nobility! The old scoundrel! (*He rises, inflamed by his thoughts, and orates in his best revolutionary manner.*) Citoyen—citizens. Will you tolerate forever these privileged ones, this old nobility protected by the kings of France? This class whose rights spring from neither nature nor reason but from tyranny—this class of courtiers—these usurpers of free lands by might, not right—— Oh—— (*A well dressed man of about thirty appears in the doorway and, unseen by* VITEK, *watches him a moment.*)

GREGOR.   Good day, Citizen Marat.

VITEK (*still in the full heat of his oratory*).   No, no. That's not Marat; that's Danton: the oration of the twenty-third of October, seventeen ninety-two. (*Suddenly realizing who is present, he again becomes* VITEK, *the clerk.*) I beg a thousand pardons, Sir.

GREGOR.   Isn't the Doctor here?

VITEK (*hastily climbing down the ladder*).   No, Sir, he hasn't come back yet, Sir.

GREGOR.   And the verdict?

VITEK.   I don't know, Sir. It's a shame—such a good case, Sir.

GREGOR.   Is it lost?

VITEK.   That I don't know; the Doctor has been in court all morning, but—I—should——

GREGOR (*throwing himself into the armchair*).   Telephone the court! Ask for Dr. Kolonaty. Hurry!

VITEK (*running to the telephone*).   Yes, Sir. Right

away, Sir. Hello——? I shouldn't have carried it to the Supreme Court, Sir.

GREGOR. Why?

VITEK. Because—Hello——? Two-two-three-five—yes —three-five—yes. (*He turns round*) Because it means the end, Sir!

GREGOR. The end?

VITEK (*forgetting the telephone*). The end of the case of Gregor vs. Prus. Why, Sir, it wasn't any longer just a case. It had become an historical monument—— Just think, it has lasted for over ninety—— (*Into the telephone*) Hello. Yes, Miss. This is Dr. Kolonaty's office. I'd like to speak with the Doctor. Yes, this is his office. (*He turns round.*) Gregor vs. Prus. Yes indeed—that's a piece of history. Almost one hundred years—(*Into the telephone*) Hello——? Has he gone? Oh, thank you. (*He hangs up the receiver.*) He's already left. He's probably on his way over here.

GREGOR. And the verdict——?

VITEK. I wish I could tell you, Sir, but I don't know. I wish there weren't going to be one! I can't help it, Mr. Gregor. But when I think that this is the last day of the case of Gregor vs. Prus—Why, I've been writing on it for thirty-four years, that was when your deceased father— God rest his soul—used to come here. Ah, he and the deceased Dr. Kolonaty, this one's father—that was a great generation, Sir. (*The old clerk sighs as he recalls past glories.*)

GREGOR. Indeed.

VITEK. Great lawyers, Sir—Why, for thirty years they kept up this case, Sir—appeals and such clever tricks. But you—boom—straight to the highest court—and that ends it! It's too bad. Such a beautiful case. And to kill a hundred-year case—like *that*.

GREGOR.   Don't, Vitek. I want to win it.

VITEK.   Or lose it, Sir?

GREGOR.   I'd rather lose it than—be this way—— Listen, Vitek. It's maddening! To have a hundred and fifty million under your nose all the time, almost to have your hands on it. To hear of nothing else all your life. (*He stands up.*) Do you think I shall lose?

VITEK.   I don't know, Mr. Gregor. Very doubtful case, Sir.

GREGOR.   Very well. If I lose, then——

VITEK.   You will shoot yourself, Sir? Your deceased father used to talk just the same way.

GREGOR.   And he shot himself.

VITEK.   But not because of the case—his debts. When one lives that way—on his prospects—

GREGOR (*dropping back into the chair*).   Oh, be quiet, I beg of you.

VITEK.   Oh, you haven't nerve enough for a big case. And such beautiful material, too. (*He climbs up the ladder and takes out the Gregor papers.*) Just look at these briefs, Mr. Gregor. Eighteen twenty-seven, the oldest number in our office. Unique, Sir. It ought to be in a museum. And look at the beautiful handwriting of eighteen forty. Lord, that man had a hand! Why, Sir, I tell you it's a pleasure to look at it.

GREGOR.   Oh, you are a fool—let me alone.

VITEK (*putting back the papers piously*).   Well, well. Perhaps the Supreme Court will still put it off. (*A demure young girl, who at eighteen still wears her hair down, quietly opens the door.*)

KRISTINA.   Papa, aren't you coming home?

VITEK (*climbing down the ladder*). Right away. Right away. As soon as the Doctor gets back.

GREGOR (*standing up*). Your daughter?

VITEK. Oh, yes. Stay outside, Kristina. Wait for me in the corridor.

GREGOR. Oh, please don't, that is, not on my account. (*To* KRISTINA.) Are you coming from school?

KRISTINA. No, from a rehearsal.

VITEK. My daughter sings in the theater. Now run along, Kristina. There's nothing you can do here.

KRISTINA. Papa, she is mar-vel-ous!

GREGOR. Who?

KRISTINA. Why, Mademoiselle Marty, of course. Emilia Marty.

GREGOR. Emilia Marty?

KRISTINA. She is the greatest singer in the world. You know she's singing tonight, and this morning she rehearsed with us. (*A thought comes to her and she runs over to* VITEK.) Oh, Papa!

VITEK. Yes?

KRISTINA. Papa, I—I'm going to leave the theater. I don't want to keep on—not for anything. Not for anything. (*She sobs and turns her back.*)

VITEK. Why, Kristina, what have they done to you?

KRISTINA. Oh, it isn't that, it's because—I know so little. Oh, Papa, Mademoiselle Marty—I—if you could hear her, you'd understand. I don't ever want to sing again.

VITEK. Will you listen to that! And she has a lovely voice, too. Silly girl! There, there!

GREGOR. Who knows, perhaps the famous Marty would envy you.

KRISTINA. Envy me. What for?

GREGOR. Your youth.

VITEK. Of course. Of course, so you see, Krista—this is Mr. Gregor, you know—wait till you're as old as she. How old is this Marty?

KRISTINA. I don't know. It's hard to tell. About thirty.

VITEK. You see, thirty. She's old.

KRISTINA. But she's beautiful. You can't imagine how beautiful she is!

VITEK. Well, thirty years! Just wait. When you're—

GREGOR. This evening I shall go to the theater, but not to see Marty—I shall go to see you.

KRISTINA. You'll be foolish not to look at Marty all the time—and blind, too. (*Realizing her audacity, she stops. Then, to cover her confusion, she curtseys.*) But I thank you, just the same.

VITEK. That's enough. (*To* GREGOR) Oh, she's such a silly little goose.

KRISTINA. Well, he ought not to talk about Marty if he hasn't seen her. Everyone's crazy about her. Everyone!

KOLONATY (*entering briskly*). Why, here's Kristina. How do you do, Kristina. Ah, and my client. How are you?

GREGOR. How did we come out?

KOLONATY (*handing his hat and coat to* VITEK). We didn't. The Supreme Court adjourned.

GREGOR. For another conference?

KOLONATY. No, for dinner.

GREGOR. And the verdict?

KOLONATY. Not till this afternoon. My dear Sir, you must have patience. Have you had your dinner?

VITEK. Oh, Lord, Lord!

KOLONATY. What is it?

VITEK. Too bad! Such a beautiful case!

GREGOR (*sitting down*). To wait again. Oh!

KRISTINA. Come on, Papa.

KOLONATY. Well, Kristina, and how are you getting along? It's nice to see you again.

GREGOR. Tell me frankly, what are our chances?

KOLONATY. La, la.

GREGOR. But?

KOLONATY. Listen, my friend. Did I ever give you any hopes?

GREGOR. Then why are you——?

KOLONATY. Why am I carrying on this case for you? Why? Because I inherited you, my friend. You, Vitek, and that desk over there. What do you expect? Gregor vs. Prus is a family inheritance—like a disease. And it doesn't cost you a cent.

GREGOR. You'll get paid after I win the case.

KOLONATY. Oh, yes, how nice that will be.

GREGOR. You think, then, we will lose?

KOLONATY. Of course.

GREGOR (*crushed for the moment*). All right.

KOLONATY. Well, you don't have to shoot yourself yet.

KRISTINA. Papa!

GREGOR (*mastering himself*). Oh, no. Tonight I am going to the theater to see you, Miss Kristina.

KRISTINA. Not me. (*The bell rings.*)

VITEK. What, someone else? I'll say you're not here. (*He goes out.*)

KOLONATY. My, my, Kristina, how you have grown! In a very short time, you will be a great lady.

KRISTINA (*who has been watching GREGOR all the time.*) Look!

KOLONATY. What?

KRISTINA. Mr. Gregor. How pale he looks.

GREGOR. I beg your pardon. I'm not feeling well.

VITEK (*behind the door*).   In here, Madam. Yes, please. Enter, please. This way—— (EMILIA MARTY *sweeps grandly into the office—a tall, strangely beautiful woman. What so many lesser actresses try to be, she is: cold but dazzling, unique, impelling, mysterious, and always at ease.*)

KRISTINA.   It's Marty!

EMILIA (*standing in the doorway*).   Dr. Kolonaty?

KOLONATY.   Yes. What can I do for you?

EMILIA.   I am Emilia Marty. I came to see you about——

KOLONATY (*with a deep bow he shows her a seat*). Won't you, please?

EMILIA.   Thank you. (*She advances into the room.*) I came to see you about—the Gregor case.

GREGOR.   What's that, Madam Marty?

EMILIA.   I am not married.

KOLONATY.   Mademoiselle Marty, this is Mr. Gregor, my client.

EMILIA.   This one? (*She looks intently at him.*) Very well. He can stay if he wants to. (*She sits down.*)

VITEK (*pushing* KRISTINA *out through the doorway*). Now, come along, Kristina. (*He leaves on tip-toe, bowing.*)

EMILIA.   I've seen that girl somewhere.

KOLONATY (*closing the door*).   Mademoiselle Marty, this is a great honor.

EMILIA.   Not at all. So you are the lawyer?

KOLONATY.   At your service.

EMILIA.   And you represent this Mr. Gregor?

GREGOR.   Why, of course.

EMILIA.   In the case concerning the inheritance of Pepi Prus.

KOLONATY.   That is, of Baron Joseph Ferdinand Prus, deceased eighteen hundred and twenty-seven.

EMILIA.   What! Is he dead?

KOLONATY.   I'm sorry to say, almost a hundred years ago.

EMILIA.   Oh, the poor thing. I didn't know that.

KOLONATY.   Oh, is that so? (*Sharply*) And is there anything else I can do for you?

EMILIA (*She rises to leave*).   I don't want to take up your time.

KOLONATY (*also rising*).   I beg your pardon. I hardly think you'd come here without some reason.

EMILIA.   No. (*She sits down again.*) There is something I wanted to tell you.

KOLONATY (*sitting down*).   Concerning the Gregor case?

EMILIA.   Yes.

KOLONATY.   But aren't you a stranger?

EMILIA.   Yes, of course. I only learned this morning about your—about this gentleman's case. Purely by chance.

KOLONATY.   Really!

EMILIA.   Only from the newspapers. I was reading what they had written about me and all at once I saw: "The last day of the case: Gregor vs. Prus." Coincidence, wasn't it?

KOLONATY.   Well, it was in all the newspapers.

EMILIA.   And because—by accident—I remembered something—but first, won't you tell me some of the particulars of the case?

KOLONATY.   Certainly. Ask me any questions you like.

EMILIA.   I don't know anything about it.

KOLONATY.   Nothing at all? Not a word?

EMILIA.   It's the first time I have heard of it—really.

KOLONATY.   But then—pardon me—I don't understand —why you are interested.

GREGOR.   Tell her the story, Doctor.

KOLONATY.   Well, it's a very old case.

EMILIA.   Gregor's in the right, isn't he?

KOLONATY.   Probably, but even so, that won't help him.

GREGOR.   Tell her about it.

EMILIA.   Please do.

KOLONATY.   Well, if it interests you. (*He leans back in his armchair and talks rapidly.*) Now, from eighteen hundred and twenty on, in the baronial estate of Prus; that is, in the estates of Semonix, Loukov, Nova, Ves, Konigsdord and so on, a feeble-minded baron, Joseph Ferdinand Prus—

EMILIA.   Pepi—feeble-minded? No, no!

KOLONATY.   Well, then, let us say eccentric.

EMILIA (*strangely insistent*).   No—— Say unfortunate

KOLONATY.   Pardon me. You can't be certain.

EMILIA.   You, even less.

KOLONATY.   Well, anyway—Joseph Ferdinand Prus died childless and without a will, in the year eighteen hundred and twenty-seven.

EMILIA.   What did he die of?

KOLONATY.   Inflammation of the brain, or something like that. His cousin, the Polish Baron Emmerich Prus, came into the inheritance. And a certain Ferdinand Karel Gregor, otherwise great-grandfather of my client, entered a claim on the property of Loukov.

EMILIA.   When?

KOLONATY.   Just after his death in eighteen twenty-seven.

EMILIA. But at that time Ferdinand must still have been a little boy.

KOLONATY. Quite right. At that time he was a pupil in the Teresan Academy. He was represented by a Viennese lawyer. His claim on the property of Loukov was based on these facts: That the deceased, one year before his death, came to the director of the Teresan Academy and declared that he was giving to Ferdinand Karel Gregor the aforesaid estate, along with the castle, farms, dairies and inventory. The income from the aforesaid property to be used for the education of the aforesaid minor, Gregor, which aforesaid must, as soon as he becomes of age, take over the full ownership of the aforesaid property, item of fact *pro secundo*. The aforesaid minor received from the owner during the lifetime of the deceased the income and reports from the aforesaid property with the title of owner and possessor of the property of Loukov. Of which proof is given by possession. (*He pauses for effect and also to catch his breath.*)

EMILIA. Well, that seems to order, doesn't it?

KOLONATY (*again warming to his subject*). Wait. Against that, Baron Emmerich Prus protested that the donation of the aforesaid property was not recorded in the land record, that the deceased did not leave behind any written will, but, that in eighteen twenty-seven, at his country estate, made an oral "last will" for the benefit of another person.

EMILIA. It isn't possible. What other person?

KOLONATY. There's the hitch, Madam. Wait, I'll read the whole thing. (*He climbs up the ladder by the pigeon-hole file.*) It is very amusing, you'll see. Here it is. (*He takes out the Gregor papers, sits down on the bottom step and quickly fingers them.*) B-z-z-z. Here, "The record of the life of the high-born city councilor nobleman: Prus, Joseph Ferdinand von Semonitz." Will: the record at death-bed which was signed by a priest, a doctor and a notary. Here—"The dying—in high fever—asked by the undersigned if he had some last wish, declared several times that the property of Loukov should go to Mr. Mach Gregor." To Mr. Mach, comma, Gregor. (*He puts back the papers.*)—To some Mr. Mach, Madam—to some Gregor Mach—to a person then unknown and undiscoverable. (*He remains seated on the ladder.*)

EMILIA. That is a mistake. Pepi certainly meant Gregor, Ferdi Gregor.

KOLONATY. Apparently. But what is written is written. At that time the above-named Gregor protested that the word "Mach" appeared in the oral will only by some mistake of hearing or slip of the pen; that "Gregor" should have been the last name, not the first name, and so on; but *litera scripta valet.* And Emmerich Prus kept Loukov and the whole inheritance.

EMILIA. And Gregor?

KOLONATY. Gregor got nothing.

GREGOR. You see, Madam, this is called justice.

EMILIA. But why didn't Gregor get it?

KOLONATY. Well, dear lady, for various technical reasons and chiefly because neither Gregor Mach nor Ferdinand Karel Gregor was a blood relation of the deceased.

EMILIA. But wait. He was his son.

KOLONATY. Whose son?

EMILIA. Ferdinand Gregor was Pepi's son.

GREGOR (*jumping up*). His son! How do you know that?

KOLONATY (*coming hastily down the ladder*). His son? And who was the mother, please?

EMILIA. The mother was—her name was Ellian Mac-Gregor, a singer at the Viennese court opera.

GREGOR (*excitedly*). What did you say her name was?

EMILIA. MacGregor. You know, it is a Scotch name.

GREGOR. MacGregor, do you hear, Doctor? Mac. Mac. Not Mach. Do you understand?

KOLONATY (*still doubtful*). Of course. But why, Madam, wasn't her son's name also MacGregor?

EMILIA. Well, because of his mother—Ferdi never knew his own mother.

KOLONATY. Ah, is that so? (*Coming closer to her*) And have you any proof of this?

EMILIA. I'm not sure. Please go on.

KOLONATY. Well, from that time the Loukov case has been going on, with some intervals, up to the present date. It has been carried on continuously for a hundred years between generations of the Pruses and the Gregors and with the excellent legal assistance of the Doctors Kolonaty. Thanks to their help, the last of the Gregors will lose it for good. Oddly enough, this very afternoon. So—that is all.

EMILIA. And is Loukov worth so much trouble?

GREGOR. I should say so.

KOLONATY. In the sixties coal was found on the Loukov property. The price cannot be estimated, even approximately—but let us say one hundred and fifty millions.

EMILIA. Anything more?

GREGOR. No, nothing more. That would be quite enough for me.

KOLONATY. Now, my dear lady, have you any more questions?

EMILIA. Yes. What do you need to win the case?

KOLONATY (*with a touch of sarcastic humor*). Well, of course, I should like best of all to have the true, written will.

EMILIA. And do you know of one?

KOLONATY. We found none.

EMILIA. That was careless.

KOLONATY. Unquestionably. (*He gets up.*) Any more questions?

EMILIA. Yes. To whom does the old Prus house belong?

GREGOR. To my opponent, Jaroslav Prus.

EMILIA. And what are those cabinets where you put wills called?

GREGOR. Archives.

KOLONATY. Files.

EMILIA. Then listen. (*They approach her. She speaks rapidly in a low voice.*) In the Prus house there used to be such a cabinet. Every drawer had a date and there Pepi used to put bills and other old papers. Do you follow me?

KOLONATY. Yes.

EMILIA. And on one of the drawers there was the date, eighteen hundred and sixteen. In that year Pepi met Ellian MacGregor during the Congress at Vienna.

KOLONATY. I see.

EMILIA. And in one of the drawers he hid all his letters from Ellian.

KOLONATY (*coming closer to her*). And how do you know that?

EMILIA. You must not ask me.

KOLONATY (*with an over-elaborate bow*). Pardon me.

EMILIA. There are also letters from the managers and people like that, you know. In short, a lot of old papers.

KOLONATY. Yes.

EMILIA. Do you think they've been burned?

KOLONATY. Perhaps. It is quite possible.

EMILIA. Well, will you find out?

KOLONATY. Of course, provided Mr. Prus will allow me.

EMILIA. And if he doesn't?

KOLONATY. What can we do?

EMILIA. You will have to get the drawer open some other way. (*She stands close to him, looking him straight in the eyes.*) Do you understand?

KOLONATY. Oh, yes, I suppose, at midnight with a rope ladder and a skeleton key and all that. My dear lady, you certainly have queer ideas about us lawyers.

EMILIA. But you must get it.

KOLONATY. Well, we shall see. Anything else?

EMILIA. If those letters are there you will find among them a big, yellow envelope.

KOLONATY. And in it?

EMILIA. The last will of Prus, written in his own hand and sealed. (KOLONATY *and* GREGOR *both leap to their feet.*)

KOLONATY. My God!

GREGOR. Are you sure?

KOLONATY (*now for the first time carried away by* EMILIA'*s story*). What's in it? What does it say?

EMILIA. Well, in it Pepi leaves the estate of Loukov to his illegitimate son Ferdinand, born in Loukov at such and such a time. I have forgotten the date.

KOLONATY. In those very words?

EMILIA. In those very words.

KOLONATY. And is the envelope sealed?

EMILIA. Yes.

KOLONATY. With the original seal of Joseph Prus?

EMILIA. Yes.

KOLONATY. Ah—— (*He looks at* EMILIA *and laughs.*)
Thank you. (*He sits down.*) Would you mind telling me,
my dear lady, why you're making such fools of us?

EMILIA. Oh—you don't believe me?

KOLONATY. I should say not. Not a word.

GREGOR. I believe her. How can you tell——?

KOLONATY. Be sensible. If the envelope is sealed how
can anyone tell what is in it?

GREGOR. But——

KOLONATY. In an envelope sealed for a hundred years.

GREGOR. Just the same——

KOLONATY. And in a strange house. (*Losing his patience.*) Don't be an idiot!

GREGOR. But I do believe her, and that's all.

KOLONATY. As you wish. My dear Miss Marty, you
have an extraordinary weakness for telling stories. Do you
suffer from it often?

GREGOR. Oh, stop.

KOLONATY. Very well. I won't say another word. Ab-
solute secrecy, my dear lady.

GREGOR (*now quite enraged at the Doctor*). And if you
want to know, Doctor, I believe every word she said.

EMILIA. At least you are a gentleman.

GREGOR. And, therefore, either you go to his house and
ask for the papers of eighteen-sixteen——

KOLONATY. Or?

GREGOR. Or I am going to get the services of the first
lawyer I find in the telephone book and shall hand over
the case to him.

KOLONATY (*completely taken aback*). ——For my
sake!

GREGOR. All right. (*He goes to the telephone and looks through the telephone book.*)

KOLONATY. Stop this foolishness! We're friends, aren't we? I used to be your guardian.

GREGOR. Dr. Abeles, Alfred, two-seven-six-one.

KOLONATY. Man, don't take that fellow. That's my last advice, unless you want to be absolutely ruined.

GREGOR (*at the telephone*). Hello—two-siven-six-one?

KOLONATY. Don't disgrace us. You're not going to give our hereditary case to such——?

GREGOR. Dr. Abeles? This is Albert Gregor speaking——

KOLONATY (*snatching the receiver from his ear*). Wait. I'll go.

GREGOR. To Prus?

KOLONATY. To the devil if you like, but you stay here.

GREGOR. Doctor, if you're not back in one hour I am going to call——

KOLONATY. Shut up! I beg your pardon, my dear lady. And, if you please, don't make him entirely crazy. (*Runs out.*)

GREGOR. At last.

EMILIA. Is he really such a fool?

GREGOR. No. He's only practical. He doesn't know what to do with miracles. I always waited for a miracle, and you came. Oh, how can I thank you?

EMILIA. It isn't worth the words.

GREGOR (*he sits down*). You know, I'm almost certain that the will will be found. I don't know why I have such faith now (*he gazes up at her a moment in silence*) perhaps because you are so beautiful.

EMILIA. How old are you?

GREGOR. Thirty-four, Mademoiselle Marty. From my

childhood I lived only to get those millions. You can't imagine what it was. I lived like a fool. I didn't know any better. If you hadn't come—

EMILIA.   Debts?

GREGOR.   Yes. (*He rises.*) Tonight I would have shot myself, probably.

EMILIA.   Nonsense!

GREGOR (*more and more under her spell*).   I won't hide anything from you, dear lady. There was no help for me and all at once you came. Lord knows from where. Famous singer—a mysterious woman—to save me. (*She laughs*) Why do you laugh at me?

EMILIA (*pushing him back*).   You talk such rubbish!

GREGOR.   But——? Dear lady, we are alone now. You're fascinating. Speak! Tell me everything!

EMILIA.   What more? I've said enough.

GREGOR.   This is a family matter. There are some family secrets. You know about them in some extraordinary way. In God's name, tell me evertyhing.

EMILIA (*shaking her head*).   No.

GREGOR.   You can't?

EMILIA (*walking away from him*).   I don't want to.

GREGOR (*following her*).   How do you know about those letters? How do you know about the last will? Where from? How long ago? Who told you all this? Don't you see, I've got to know what's behind it. Who are you? What does it all mean?

EMILIA.   A miracle.

GREGOR.   Yes, a miracle. But even a miracle has to be explained, or it's unbearable. Why did you come?

EMILIA.   To help you, as you see.

GREGOR.   Why do you want to help me? Why me? What is there in it for you?

EMILIA. That's my affair.

GREGOR. Mine, also, Mademoiselle Marty. If I am to owe this property—even my life—to you, what may I lay at your feet?

EMILIA. What do you mean?

GREGOR. What may I offer you, Miss Marty?

EMILIA (*playing with him*). Oh, I see. You want to pay me—what do you call it?—a percentage.

GREGOR. Now, please. Use some other word. Call it gratitude. How could I spend——?

EMILIA. I have enough myself.

GREGOR. Excuse me. Only a beggar could have enough. The rich, never.

EMILIA. Look here! You good-for-nothing boy, stop offering me money!

GREGOR. Excuse me. I'm afraid I don't know how to offer gifts. (*He gets down on his knees*) Lady, they call you the divine Marty, but in this world of ours, even a divinity would ask for a share. It's only right. Understand, I speak of millions.

EMILIA. You're giving it away already. Oh, you little fool! (*She goes to the window and looks out.*)

GREGOR (*getting up and coming to the front of the stage.*) Why do you speak to me as though I were a boy? I'd give half my inheritance if——

EMILIA. Well?

GREGOR. It's unbearable how small I feel beside you! (*Pause*)

EMILIA (*turning round*). What is your name?

GREGOR. I beg your pardon?

EMILIA. What is your name?

GREGOR. Gregor.

EMILIA. The rest?

GREGOR. MacGregor.

EMILIA. But your first name, idiot?

GREGOR. Albert.

EMILIA. Your mother calls you Berti, doesn't she?

GREGOR. Yes, but my mother is dead.

EMILIA. Bah! (*She turns away in disgust.*) Everyone is just dying. (*There is a pause.*)

GREGOR. What was Ellian MacGregor like?

EMILIA. At last, it has occurred to you to ask about her.

GREGOR. Do you know something about her? Who was she?

EMILIA. A great singer.

GREGOR. Was she beautiful?

EMILIA. She was.

GREGOR. Did she love my great-grandfather?

EMILIA. Yes, in her way.

GREGOR. Where did she die?

EMILIA. I don't know. Enough of this. One more thing—— (*Pause*)

GREGOR (*coming near her*). Emilia.

EMILIA. I am not Emilia to you.

GREGOR (*in a sudden burst of passion*). What am I to you? For God's sake, don't torture me. Don't play with me. You're a beautiful, fascinating woman. (*He takes her by the shoulders and gazes down into her face*) Listen, I understand you. (*She laughs*) No, don't laugh at me. Oh, you're wonderful—superb.

EMILIA. I'm not laughing, Berti. But don't be a fool!

GREGOR. I am a fool! And I'm glad! You've stirred me to the soul. Have you ever seen blood—running blood? The sight of it makes one savage—wild—drives a man to madness. Men must have gone mad that way over you.

Listen—(*His hands slip up round her throat. There is menace in his voice.*) I can't understand—I can't understand why someone hasn't taken hold of you—and strangled you! (*His fingers close tighter and tighter round her throat.* EMILIA *struggles and wrenches herself away.*)

EMILIA. Ah, don't start that.

GREGOR. But I must speak. You are cold to me. That hurts. The moment you came in, you scorched me like a hot flame. What is it? You bring something terrible; has anyone ever told you that?—Emilia, do you know how beautiful you are?

EMILIA (*in a tired way*). Beautiful? No. Look!

GREGOR. Oh, God! What are you doing? What are you doing to your face? (*He steps back.*) Emilia, don't do it! Stop! Now—you look old. (*Covering his eyes with his hands, he sinks back into a chair.*) Terrible!

EMILIA. Now you see. Go, Berti. Leave me. (*There is a pause.*)

GREGOR. Excuse me. I was a—oh, I don't know what I am doing.

EMILIA. Berti, do I really look very old?

GREGOR (*lifting his head to look at her*). No, not now. No, you are terribly beautiful.

EMILIA. Do you know what you could give me?

GREGOR. What?

EMILIA. You offered me yourself. Do you know what I want?

GREGOR. Everything I have is yours.

EMILIA. Listen, Berti. Do you know Greek?

GREGOR. No.

EMILIA. Well, then, give me the Greek papers. They're no use to you.

GREGOR. Greek papers?

EMILIA. The ones Ferdi got. You know, Berti. From your great-grandfather, Pepi Prus. They were just a remembrance—— Will you give them to me?

GREGOR. I don't know of any Greek papers.

EMILIA. Nonsense! You must have them. Pepi promised that he would give them to him. For the love of God, Berti, tell me you have them!

GREGOR. But I haven't them!

EMILIA (*turning sharply on him*). Don't lie. You must have them.

GREGOR (*rising*). I have not.

EMILIA. Fool! I want them. I have to have them, do you hear? You must find them!

GREGOR. Where are they?

EMILIA. How do I know? Look for them! Bring them here! Why, that is why I came here today, Berti.

GREGOR. Yes?

EMILIA. Where are they? For God's sake, think!

GREGOR. Hasn't Prus got them?

EMILIA. Take them away from him. Help me! Help me! (*The telephone rings.*)

GREGOR. Just a minute. (*He answers the telephone.*)

EMILIA (*sinking into a chair*). Find them! Find them!

GREGOR (*at the telephone*). Hello. This is Dr. Kolonaty's office. He isn't here. Is there any message? This is Gregor speaking. Yes. All right. Good. Thank you very much. (*He hangs up the receiver.*) That's over.

EMILIA. What?

GREGOR. The case of Gregor vs. Prus. The Supreme Court has brought in a verdict.

EMILIA. And?

GREGOR. I lost. (*Pause*)

EMILIA. Couldn't your fool of a lawyer have held it up for a while? (GREGOR *shrugs his shoulders.*) But you can still appeal, can't you?

GREGOR. I don't know. I don't think so.

EMILIA. That's absurd! (*She goes over to him and speaks in a motherly way.*) Listen, Berti, I'm going to pay your debts. Do you understand?

GREGOR. Why should you? I don't want you to.

EMILIA. Be quiet! I'm going to pay them and that is all there is to it. But you must help me find those Greek papers.

GREGOR (*again caught up by his desire*). Emilia——

EMILIA (*starting for the door*). Call my car, please. (DR. KOLONATY *enters in great excitement,* BARON PRUS *behind him.*)

KOLONATY. We found it! We found it! (*He throws himself before* EMILIA *on his knee.*) Gracious lady, accept my apologies. I am a stupid old fool and you know everything.

PRUS (*shaking hands with* GREGOR). I congratulate you on finding the true will.

GREGOR. Please don't. You've just won the case yourself.

PRUS. But you are going to appeal?

KOLONATY (*rising*). Of course, we will appeal.

PRUS. Will you introduce me, please?

KOLONATY. Pardon, Mademoiselle Marty—Baron Prus, my client's enemy. (THE BARON *steps forward, takes her outstretched hand and raises it to his lips.*)

EMILIA. I am very pleased to meet you. Where are the letters?

PRUS (*as though he did not understand*). Letters?

EMILIA.   From Ellian.

PRUS.   Oh, I have them. Mr. Gregor need not trouble himself about them.

EMILIA.   Will they come to him?

PRUS.   If he inherits the property. As a remembrance of Miss—— (*He smirks at his intentional slip.*)—er—his great-grandmother.

EMILIA.   Listen, you will return those letters to me, won't you?

PRUS.   Return? Have they ever been yours?

EMILIA.   Oh, no. But Berti was going to give them to me.

PRUS.   I see. (*And the* BARON *undoubtedly does see many things which have not been spoken.*) And, now, for showing me what I have in my house, I should like to offer you this beautiful bouquet.

EMILIA.   You are not very generous. Berti offered me——

PRUS.   A wagon-load?

EMILIA.   No, but I don't know how many millions.

PRUS.   And you took them?

EMILIA.   Hardly.

PRUS.   You did well. (*He looks at her intently.*) Don't ever take anything you can't be sure of.

EMILIA.   Ah—is there anything the matter?

PRUS.   Well, perhaps just a little trifle. Is his great-grandfather Gregor the Ferdinand Gregor of the will? You know these lawyers are really very exact.

EMILIA.   You need another little document?

PRUS.   Just that.

EMILIA (*turning to* KOLONATY). All right, Doctor, I shall send you something like that tomorrow morning.

KOLONATY (*who has been eagerly following the conver-*

sation). What? You have it? Gregor! We will win our case after all!

PRUS.   Mademoiselle Marty, I think you had better take my gift.

EMILIA (*looking first at* GREGOR, *then at* PRUS). Why?

PRUS.   It's surer. (*She takes the bouquet and, as* PRUS *bows over her hand, the curtain falls.*)

ACT II

(The stage of a big theater, somewhat in disorder after the previous night's performance. Properties, scenery, rolled drops and lighting apparatus are left about the stage. In the front is a theatrical throne on a dais.)

SCRUBWOMAN *(pausing in her work)*. I tell you that was glory. Did you see the flowers?

MECHANIC. I should say I did.

SCRUBWOMAN. As long as I've lived I never seen such glories. The people yelled. I thought they'd tear down the theater. And Marty had to go about fifty times to bow. The people wouldn't stop. Just as if they was crazy.

MECHANIC. Listen. She must have a lot of money.

SCRUBWOMAN. I should say so, Kudrana. Only think of the money them flowers cost. Look! Look! *(She points to a heap of flowers carelessly tossed into a corner.)* There's another heap. She couldn't take them all away with her.

MECHANIC. Well, I came to listen a little while behind the stage, but you know I just tremble all over when she sings.

SCRUBWOMAN. I tell you this, Kudrana, I just cries. I listened, and all at once I wondered what was running down my cheeks, and there I was, crying. *(PRUS enters from the back. He wanders about as if looking for someone, then finally comes down to the SCRUBWOMAN.)*

SCRUBWOMAN *(getting up)*. Do you want to see someone?

36

PRUS. Isn't Mademoiselle Marty here? They told me at the hotel she's gone to the theater.

SCRUBWOMAN. She's with the manager now, but she'll be back here. She left her things in her dressing room.

PRUS. Good. I'll wait. (*He steps aside.*)

SCRUBWOMAN. That's the fifth one. There's a whole string of 'em waiting for her.

MECHANIC. I can't get it into my head that such a woman can be bothered with men.

SCRUBWOMAN (*with a knowing wag of the head*). Oh, yes, there's no doubt about it, Kudrana.

MECHANIC. You don't say.

SCRUBWOMAN. What—what are you staring at?

MECHANIC. I can't get it into my head. (*He goes "up stage" pausing to hear her reply, then goes off.*)

SCRUBWOMAN. Of course she has! But you're too stupid to understand. (*She picks up her pail and mop and disappears among the "flats" and "properties" at the back of the stage.*)

KRISTINA (*entering from the left*). Janek, come here. Janek, there's no one here.

JANEK (*Timidly following her*). Won't somebody throw me out?

KRISTINA. No one rehearses today. Oh, dear! Janek, I'm so unhappy!

JANEK. Why? (*He tries to kiss her.*)

KRISTINA. No, Janek, don't kiss me—please—I have other cares now. I mustn't think of you any more.

JANEK. But, Krista!

KRISTINA. Be sensible, Janek. If I'm to get anywhere, I must change my whole life. (*Very seriously*) Janek, if one thinks all the time about some one thing, and only about the same thing, it must come true, mustn't it?

JANEK. Of course.

KRISTINA. So, you see. I have to think only about my art. (*She mounts the throne and sits down.*) Marty is marvelous, isn't she, Janek?

JANEK. She is, but——

KRISTINA. You don't understand. It's her marvelous technique. I didn't sleep the whole night. I lay on my back and wondered and wondered whether I should leave the theater or not. If I could know only just a little bit.

JANEK. But you do. (*He follows her and sits on the arm of the throne.*)

KRISTINA. Do you really think so? Do you think I ought to go on singing? Then everything would have to end between us. You understand. I should have to give all my time to the stage.

JANEK. But, Krista, a few minutes every day—twice a day—with me.

KRISTINA. That's just it. It isn't only a few minutes. Oh, it's terrible! You know, Janek, I think about you the whole day. Oh, what a nuisance you are! How can I do anything I ought to when I think about you all the time?

JANEK. And if you want to know, Krista, I—I—can think of nothing but you.

KRISTINA. It's all right for you. You don't have to sing, and, oh, listen, Janek, I've dreamed of triumphs and glories—so you mustn't hope.

JANEK. I will hope! I won't agree to this—I——

KRISTINA. Please, Janek, don't make it more difficult. Be sensible, dear. I'd have to give up any serious study, and then, oh, I don't want to be a poor girl always—for your sake—and then, my voice is only being formed. I ought not to use it too much.

JANEK. Then I'll do the talking.

KRISTINA.   No, wait! I have decided. It is all over between us, Janek. All over! (JANEK *jumps up and is half-
way off the stage before she continues*) . . . We're going
to see each other only once a day. (*He stops and turns
round.*)

JANEK.   But——

KRISTINA.   Between times, we must be perfect strangers.
I'm going to work terribly hard, Janek. To sing, to think,
to learn and everything. You know, I'd love to be a great
lady like Marty. Come here, you silly. There's room
enough for you beside me. Nobody's looking. Do you think
she loves someone?

JANEK (*on the throne beside her*).   Who?

KRISTINA.   She—Marty.

JANEK.   Marty? Of course.

KRISTINA.   You know, I don't understand. Why does
she have to love someone when she's so great and famous?
You don't know what it is when a woman loves. It is so
degrading!

JANEK.   It is not!

KRISTINA.   You don't know anything about it! A
woman doesn't think of herself any more. She follows him
like a slave. She can't belong to herself. Oh, I could beat
myself sometimes.

JANEK.   But——

KRISTINA.   And then everybody's crazy about Marty—
everyone she looks at. But it doesn't mean anything to her.

JANEK.   Not everyone.

KRISTINA.   I'm—afraid of her.

JANEK.   Krista! (*He tries to steal a kiss.*)

KRISTINA.   But, Janek, if somebody should see us! (*He
kisses her.* PRUS *enters and watches them.*)

PRUS.   I'm not looking.

JANEK (*jumping up*). Father!

PRUS. You don't have to run away. (*He comes nearer.*) Miss Kristina, I am very pleased to meet you. I am sorry to say I haven't known you before. The boy might at least have boasted to me about you.

KRISTINA (*stepping down from the throne and shielding JANEK*). Please, Mr. Prus just came to—to——

PRUS. Mr. Prus?

KRISTINA. Mr.—Mr.——

PRUS. He's only Janek, and not Mr. Prus. How long has he been running after you?

KRISTINA. For a year.

PRUS. Well, well! But you mustn't take him too seriously. I know him. And you, young man—I don't want to disturb you, but this is really a little—a little public, isn't it?

JANEK (*bravely stepping up to his father*). Father, if you think you'll embarrass me—you're mistaken.

PRUS. That's right. A man should never be embarrassed.

JANEK. And I never thought that you would spy on me this way.

PRUS. Bravo, Janek—only don't give in.

JANEK. I mean what I say. There are matters into which I forbid—which—are no one's——

PRUS. Quite so, my friend. Shake hands. (*His tone is harsh.*)

JANEK (*hiding his hands behind his back*). No, Father.

PRUS (*stretching out his hand*). Well?

JANEK. Father? (*He stretches out his hand timidly.*)

PRUS (*shaking hands*). That's the way.

JANEK (*His face wrinkles up. He tries to look strong. Finally he cries out and crumples up completely.*) Oh!

PRUS (*letting him go*). Well, hello. (*He laughs.*) He can stand a lot.

KRISTINA (*almost crying*). That is brutal.

PRUS (*takes her hands lightly*). Those golden hands. (VITEK *runs in.*)

VITEK. Kristina! Aha! here you are. (*He stops*) Baron Prus!

PRUS. Don't let me disturb you. (*He steps aside.*)

KRISTINA. What is it, Papa?

VITEK. You're in the newspapers, Kristina! They've written about you in the newspapers! In the write-up along with Marty. Imagine, along with Marty!

KRISTINA. Show it to me!

VITEK. Here. "The part of Ceila was sung for the first time by Miss Vitek." That's pretty nice, isn't it?

KRISTINA. And what's all the rest?

VITEK. You can just imagine—nothing but Marty. As if there were no one else in this world except Marty.

KRISTINA. Look, Janek! Here is my name.

VITEK. Krista, who is that?

KRISTINA. Mr. Prus.

JANEK. Janek Prus.

VITEK. How did you happen to meet him?

JANEK. Your daughter was kind enough——

VITEK. My daughter will tell me herself, thank you. Come, Krista. (*He stalks off with Kristina.*)

EMILIA (*She speaks off-stage*). Thank you. Thank you gentlemen. Please let me go. (*She enters and sweeps down the stage to the throne. Seeing Prus*) What, another one?

PRUS. Oh, no, Mademoiselle Marty. I don't dare to congratulate you. I came for something else.

EMILIA. But you were in the theater last night?

PRUS. To be sure.

EMILIA. Well. (*She sits on the throne.*) I don't want to see anyone else. I've had enough of it. Is that your son?

PRUS. Yes. Come here, Janek.

EMILIA. Come here, Janek, I want to see you. (*He steps up shyly.*) You were in the theater last night?

JANEK. Yes.

EMILIA. Did you like me?

JANEK. Yes.

EMELIA (*sharply*). Do you know how to say anything else but "Yes"?

JANEK. Yes.

EMILIA. Your son is stupid.

PRUS. I fear for him. (GREGOR *comes in with flowers.*)

EMILIA. Oh, Berti, bring them here.

GREGOR. For last night.

EMILIA. Let me see. (*She takes the flowers and finds a jewel box hidden in them.*) Take this back. It's nice of you to come. Thank you for the flowers. (*She takes a sniff of them and throws them carelessly on the pile with the others.*) Did you like me?

GREGOR. No. Your singing hurts me. It is too perfect. And, at the same time——

EMILIA. Well?

GREGOR. You seem bored when you sing. It is super-human. It carries one away. But you remain cold—as if you were frozen.

EMILIA. Did you feel that way? Perhaps you are right. Well, I've sent the document to your old fool of a lawyer —the one about Ellian. How is the case getting on?

GREGOR. I don't know. I don't care about the case.

(VITEK *and* KRISTINA *enter and stand silently in the background*.)

EMILIA. But you're already buying ridiculous things of the jewelers. You idiot! Take it back, right away—how did you manage to get it?

GREGOR. It's no business of yours.

EMILIA. You borrowed, didn't you? You spent the whole forenoon running from one money lender to another, eh? (*She puts her hand in her handbag and pulls out a handful of money.*) Here, take it. Quick!

GREGOR. What! Are you offering me money? What do you think I am?

EMILIA (*She stands up and comes down towards him*). Behave yourself or I shall pull your ears.

GREGOR. I hope you dare!

EMILIA. Will you only listen! Don't try to give me orders. Berti, don't make me cross. I'll teach you to run up debts. (*She boxes his ears.*) Are you going to take it?

PRUS (*to* GREGOR). In Heaven's name, put an end to this.

GREGOR (*pulling the money away from her*). You have funny whims. (*He gives the money to* VITEK.) Hand it over to the office—Mademoiselle Marty's account.

VITEK. Yes, certainly.

EMILIA. Certainly not! That is for him. Do you understand?

VITEK. Yes, certainly.

EMILIA. Were you in the theater last night? Did you like me?

VITEK. Of course, my lady. (*Attempting a compliment*) Quite a Strada.

EMILIA. Did you ever hear Strada sing? Listen. Strada shrieked. She had no voice.

VITEK. Well, Strada died a hundred years ago.

EMILIA. All the worse. You should have heard her. Strada! Why do people talk of Strada?

VITEK. I beg your pardon, I—of course I didn't hear her, but as history relates——

EMILIA (*imperiously*). Listen. History lies. I will tell you something. Strada shrieked and Carrona had a frog in her throat. Agajari was a goose and Faustina breathed like a balloon. That is history for you.

VITEK. You know best—in these matters concerning music.

PRUS. But you mustn't insult the French Revolution before Mr. Vitek.

EMILIA. Why?

PRUS. The French Revolution is his hobby.

EMILIA. What does he know about it?

PRUS. I don't know. Try asking him about Citizen Marat.

VITEK (*trying to bow himself away*). Oh, no, please.

EMILIA. Marat—wasn't he a deputy?—Hands perspired—terribly.

VITEK (*greatly incensed*). That's not true!

EMILIA. Oh, as I remember, he had hands like a frog. Br-r-r!

VITEK. Oh, no. That's a lie. It's not written anywhere. —I beg your pardon.

EMILIA. Well, I know. And what was the name of the big fellow with the pockmarks?

VITEK. Which one, please?

EMILIA. The one who had his head cut off.

VITEK. Danton?

EMILIA. Exactly! He was still worse.

PRUS. Why?

EMILIA. Oh, his teeth were completely decayed. Disgusting man! (*Everyone except* VITEK *laughs.*)

VITEK. Wait. Don't talk that way, please. That isn't historical. Danton—Danton did not have decayed teeth. That cannot be proved. And it doesn't matter the least—not the least bit.

EMILIA. Why doesn't it matter? It is disgusting.

VITEK. Now, please. You mustn't speak this way of Danton—I beg your pardon—but if you talk like that nothing noble will be left in history.

EMILIA (*rising to full height and speaking almost like an oracle*). There was nothing noble in history.

VITEK. What?

EMILIA. There never was anything very noble. *I* know.

VITEK. But Danton?

EMILIA. Just look at that—this man wants to quarrel with me.

PRUS. Insolent!

EMILIA. Oh, no. He's quite harmless. (VITEK *draws back, muttering to himself.*)

GREGOR. Shall I bring in some more people so you can be rude to them?

EMELIA. Not necessary. They will come of their own accord—on all fours.

KRISTINA. Janek, let's go.

EMILIA (*yawning*). Aren't they a pair, those two? I wonder if they've reached paradise?

VITEK. I beg your pardon?

EMILIA. I wonder if they have——

VITEK. Certainly not!

EMILIA (*calmly*). But why not? Who'd grudge them the pleasure?

VITEK (*piteously*). Krista, it isn't true, is it?

KRISTINA (*in confusion*).   But, Papa, how can you?

EMILIA.   Stop it, you fools. What wasn't will be. (*A weary tone creeps into her voice.*) And then you'll find it wasn't worth it—at all.

PRUS.   What is worth it, then?

EMILIA (*with a faraway look in her eyes. To herself*). Nothing—nothing at all. (*An old gentleman with a bouquet slowly makes his way forward. His dress is that of a man about town of a past generation. His mind, no longer vigorous, dwells in the past. Senility has laid its hand on him.*)

HAUK-SENDORF (*offering* EMILIA *the flowers*). Allow me, allow me.

EMILIA (*rousing herself*).   Now who is it?

HAUK-SENDORF.   Lady, dear lady, allow me to—(*He kneels before the throne.*) Dear lady, you look—you look —(*He sobs.*) Will you excuse——

EMILIA (*to the others*).   What's happened to him?

HAUK-SENDORF.   You—you look—so—so much like her.

EMILIA.   Like whom?

HAUK-SENDORF.   Eugenie. Eugenie Montez.

EMILIA (*She starts and gets up*).   What?

HAUK-SENDORF.   Eugenie. I—I knew her—lady—it is —it is fifty years ago.

EMILIA (*trying to cover her confusion*).   Who is this great fool?

PRUS.   Hauk-Sendorf.

EMILIA (*to herself*). Hauk-Sendorf—Max? (*She descends from the throne.*) Oh, yes, won't you get up?

HAUK-SENDORF (*rising*).   May I—may I call you Eugenie?

EMILIA (*in the kind tone one uses to children*).   You may call me anything you like. So I look like her?

HAUK-SENDORF. Look like her? Dear lady, yesterday —yesterday in the theater I thought—I thought that it was she—my Eugenie—the voice—the eyes—she used to be so beautiful—Good God! And the forehead—it startled me. (*He pauses and stands back to look at her.*) But you are taller.

EMILIA. Taller? Perhaps not.

HAUK-SENDORF. A good deal taller—Allow me. Eugenie reached me—here. I used to kiss her on her forehead.

EMILIA. And that was all?

HAUK-SENDORF. Eh? Oh—You are quite like her! Dear lady, may I give you these flowers?

EMILIA. Thanks.

HAUK-SENDORF. I could look at you forever.

EMILIA. But sit down now, dear. Berti, a chair. (*She sits down on the throne.*)

JANEK. I will get one. (*He runs after a chair.*)

KRISTINA. Not there! (*She runs after him.*)

PRUS (*to* HAUK-SENDORF). Cher comte.

HAUK-SENDORF (*steps across to him*). Well, well, well! Baron Prus! Pardon me—I didn't see you. How pleased I am. How are you?

PRUS. How are you?

HAUK-SENDORF. And how is your case? Did you get rid of that fellow?

PRUS. Oh, no. Allow me, Gregor, to introduce you.

HAUK-SENDORF. Is that Mr. Gregor? I am so pleased to meet you. How are you?

GREGOR. Well, thank you. (JANEK *and* KRISTINA *bring chairs.*)

EMILIA. Sit down, Max.

HAUK-SENDORF. Thank you very much.

EMILIA.   You sit down, too, Baron. Berti can sit on my lap.

GREGOR.   Too kind of you.

EMILIA.   If you don't want to, you can stand up.

HAUK-SENDORF.   Beautiful, divine lady. On my knees I beg your pardon.

EMILIA.   Why?

HAUK-SENDORF.   I'm an old fool. How could a woman long since dead concern you?

EMILIA.   Is she dead?

HAUK-SENDORF.   Yes.

EMILIA.   Now, that's too bad.

HAUK-SENDORF.   She has been dead for fifty years. I used to love her then—fifty years ago.

EMILIA.   Yes?

HAUK-SENDORF.   They used to call her Gitana. You know—a gypsy. And she was a gypsy. They used to call her la chula negra. That is, down there in Andalusia. At that time I was in the Embassy at Madrid. Fifty years ago —eighteen seventy.

EMILIA.   Yes?

HAUK-SENDORF.   Do you know, she sang and danced in the market places. (*The old man loses himself in his memories.*) Alza! Ola! Lord! How the whole world used to go crazy about her! Vaya. Gitana there with the castanets, you see. I was young then, and she was——

EMILIA.   ——a gypsy.

HAUK-SENDORF.   Quite so. A gypsy. Nothing but fire. Ah, God! One cannot forget. Would you believe that a man never comes to his senses? I've been a fool ever since.

EMILIA.   Oh.

HAUK-SENDORF.   I'm an idiot, lady. I am Hauk the idiot—No!—What's the word?

PRUS. Feeble-minded?

HAUK-SENDORF. Quite so. (*He nods a thanks to the* BARON.) Feeble-minded. I left everything there with her. I didn't live afterwards. It was just half living without her. But come! (*He rises unsteadily and, posturing as for a dance, plays imaginary castanets.*) Salero. Dios mio. How much you look like her. Eugenie, Eugenie! (*He cries.*)

PRUS. Hauk, be careful.

HAUK-SENDORF (*coming to himself*). I beg your pardon. I ought to be leaving.

EMILIA. I shall see you again, Max?

HAUK-SENDORF. Quite so. I shall see you again? Allow me to present my compliments. Oh, when I look at you like this——

EMILIA (*suddenly rising and hurrying down the steps, comes close to him*). Kiss me.

HAUK-SENDORF. What, eh?

EMILIA. Besa me, bobo, bobazo! (Kiss me. You big simpleton!)

HAUK-SENDORF. Jesús mil veces, Eugenia. (By a thousand heavens, Eugenia!)

EMILIA. Animal, un besito! (Stupid! Just a tiny kiss!)

HAUK-SENDORF (*Kissing her*). Eugenia, moza negra —niña—querida—carísima—— (Eugenia, my little black-eyed girl—dearie—beloved—darling.)

EMILIA. Chite, tonto! Quita! Fuera! (Hush, fool—let go, please—go! Silly.)

HAUK-SENDORF. Es ella, es ella! Gitana endiablada, ven conmigo, pronto! (It is she, it is she! My fiery gypsy. Come with me now!)

EMILIA. Ya no soy. Loco! Ahora callate! Vaya! Hasta mañana, entiendes? (Not yet, idiot! Now keep quiet.

(*Trying to get him to go*) Go! Tomorrow, do you understand, tomorrow?)

HAUK-SENDORF. Vendré, vendré mis amores! (I shall come, my love, I shall come.)

EMILIA. Vaya! (Be gone.)

HAUK-SENDORF. Ay por Dios! Cielo de Dios, es ella! Si es ella! Eugenia—— (Good Lord! By all that's holy, it *is* she! Yes, it is she—Eugenia——)

EMILIA (*pushing him*). Caramba, vaya! Fuera! (Caramba! Go! Get out!)

HAUK-SENDORF. Vendré! Madre de Dios, ella misma! (I shall come. Mother of God, it's *she* and no mistake!) (*Goes out.*)

EMILIA (*gayly*). The next one. Who wants anything from me?

VITEK. I beg your pardon, would you sign your photograph for me—that is, for Kristina?

EMILIA. Nonsense! But I will do it for Kristina. A pen! (*She signs.*) So good-by.

VITEK (*bows*). A thousand thanks. (*He goes away with* KRISTINA.)

EMILIA. The next one. Anyone else?

GREGOR. I wait till you're alone.

EMILIA. Another fool. Well, I am going.

PRUS (*stepping up*). Just one minute, please.

EMILIA. Do you want something?

PRUS (*with a slight bow*). It would seem so.

EMILIA (*yawning*). All right, out with it.

PRUS. I wanted only to ask you—you seem to know so many things about Joseph Prus.

EMILIA. Perhaps.

PRUS. Do you happen to have heard a certain name?

EMILIA. What name?

PRUS. Let's say—Makropoulos.

EMILIA (*jumping up*). What?

PRUS (*rising*). Do you know anything about Makropoulos?

EMILIA (*Trying to compose herself*). No—no. It is the first time I have heard it. Oh, go away. Go! Let me alone.

PRUS (*bowing*). I am extremely sorry.

EMILIA (*To* PRUS). Not you. You wait. There's Janek? Let him go. (JANEK *leaves. To* GREGOR) What do you want?

GREGOR. I want to talk with you.

EMILIA. I've no time for you just now.

GREGOR. I must talk to you.

EMILIA. Please, Berti, let me alone. Go, dear—now. You can come back later if you want to.

GREGOR. I will come back. (*With a slight bow to* PRUS, *he leaves.*)

EMILIA. At last.

PRUS. Excuse me, Madam. I didn't know that name would touch you so.

EMILIA. What do you know about the Makropoulos paper?

PRUS. That's what I'm asking you.

EMILIA. What do you know about the Makropoulos paper?

PRUS. Dear lady, won't you please sit down. Perhaps it will be a rather long story. (*They both sit down.*) First of all, may I ask a very intimate question—perhaps too intimate a question? (EMILIA *nods slightly.*) Have you any—particular personal interest in Mr. Gregor?

EMILIA.   No.

PRUS.   Are you very anxious to have him win the case?

EMILIA.   No.

PRUS.   Thank you. (*He leans back a moment.*) I don't want to inquire further. How do you know what is in the locked closets of my house? It is apparently your secret.

EMILIA.   Yes. Well?

PRUS.   You knew that there were certain letters. You knew that there was Prus's last will. Even that it was sealed. By the way, did you know that there was something else, besides?

EMILIA (*excitedly getting up*).   You found something there? What was it?

PRUS.   I don't know. That is what I'm asking you.

EMILIA.   You don't know what it is?

PRUS.   Do you?

EMILIA.   No.

PRUS.   I thought that Kolonaty told you. Or Gregor.

EMILIA.   Not a word.

PRUS.   Well, there was a sealed letter, and on it, in the handwriting of Joseph Prus, "For the hands of my son Ferdinand." Nothing more. That was with the last will.

EMILIA.   And you didn't open it?

PRUS.   No. It doesn't belong to me.

EMILIA.   Then give it to me.

PRUS (*rising*).   To you! Why to you?

EMILIA.   Because I want it. Because—because——

PRUS.   Well?

EMILIA.   Because I have a certain right to it.

PRUS.   May I ask what right?

EMILIA.   No. (*She walks away.*)

PRUS.   Hm! It appears—another secret of yours.

EMILIA (*She turns and comes back*).   Yes—Will you give it to me?

PRUS.   No.

EMILIA.   Very well. Then Berti shall give it to me. It belongs to him, anyway.

PRUS.   We'll see. Tell me, what's in the envelope?

EMILIA.   No. What do you know about the Makropoulos paper?

PRUS.   Another question—What do you know about Ellian MacGregor?

EMILIA.   You have her letters.

PRUS.   Perhaps you know more about it. Do you know anything else about that—courtesan?

EMILIA (*in a cold fury*).   I beg your pardon!

PRUS.   But, dear lady——

EMILIA.   How do you dare? How dare you talk that way?

PRUS.   What's the matter? How can a woman of that sort, who lived a hundred years ago, concern you?

EMILIA.   That's so—She doesn't. (*She sits down*) She was a courtesan, then?

PRUS.   I read her letters. She was a remarkable type of woman.

EMILIA.   Oh, you shouldn't have read them.

PRUS.   There are certain allusions to—extraordinary intimacies—I am not a lad, but I must confess—that her experiences in certain things——

EMILIA.   Give me those letters.

PRUS.   Perhaps you are interested—in those intimate relations.

EMILIA.   Perhaps. (*She turns and walks up to the throne and sits down.*)

PRUS (*following her*). You know what I should like to know?

EMILIA. Well?

PRUS. What you are like in love.

EMILIA. You mean things of—intimate relations?

PRUS. Perhaps.

EMILIA. Perhaps I remind you of Ellian.

PRUS. God forbid! (*He turns and steps quickly off the dais*)

EMILIA (*lightly*). Well, she was only an adventuress— licentious—that's all.

PRUS. What was her real name?

EMILIA. Ellian MacGregor. You have it on those letters.

PRUS. I beg your pardon, there is only E. M. Nothing more.

EMILIA. That, of course, means Ellian MacGregor.

PRUS. Oh no. (*Watching her closely*) It might serve just as well for other names; for instance, Emilia Marty, Eugenie Montez or a thousand other names.

EMILIA. But it is Ellian MacGregor, the Scotch singer.

PRUS (*slowly with emphasis on each word*). Or, more probably—Ellina Makropoulos, the Greek from Crete.

EMILIA. Aha! Damnation!

PRUS. Ah, hah! You knew about it, then?

EMILIA. Please; leave me in peace. (*She comes down the steps to him.*) In God's name, how do you know all this?

PRUS. Very simple. In the last letter something is said about a Ferdinand Gregor, born in Loukov, November twentieth, eighteen hundred and sixteen. I found out yesterday, and at three o'clock this morning the Dean of Loukov led me with a candle to the birth records. Poor man, he had to go in his nightshirt. And there I found it.

EMILIA.   Found what?

PRUS.   A birth record. This. (*He takes out a note book and reads.*) "Nomen infantis Ferdinand Makropoulos dies nativitatis, November twentieth, eighteen hundred and sixteen, thorus illegitimate. Father left out. Mother, Ellina Makropoulos, born in Crete."

EMILIA.   You don't know anything more?

PRUS.   Nothing. But that is enough.

EMILIA.   Poor Gregor! You will keep Loukov now, won't you?

PRUS.   At least, so long as Mr. Makropoulos doesn't come to claim it.

EMILIA.   And the sealed envelope?

PRUS.   Oh, that will be put aside for him safely.

EMILIA.   And if Mr. Makropoulos does not come?

PRUS.   Then it will remain sealed and no one will get it.

EMILIA.   Then he will come. Do you understand? And you will lose Loukov.

PRUS.   As it will please God.

EMILIA.   How can you be so stupid? (*Pause*) Come, give me the envelope.

PRUS.   Why do you keep asking me for the envelope?

EMILIA.   Makropoulos will come and get it.

PRUS.   Hm! Who is he? Where do you keep him hidden?

EMILIA.   Do you really want to know? It is Berti Gregor.

PRUS.   What! He again?

EMILIA.   Yes. Ellina Makropoulos and Ellian MacGregor were one and the same person. MacGregor was her stage name. Do you understand?

PRUS.   Perfectly. And Ferdinand Gregor was her son?

EMILIA. Yes.

PRUS. Why wasn't his name Makropoulos, then?

EMILIA. Because Ellian wanted that name to disappear from the world.

PRUS (*with an unbelieving smile*). Well, let it be so. (*He sits down.*)

EMILIA. You don't believe me?

PRUS. I didn't say that. I don't even ask how you know all this.

EMILIA. Oh, good Lord! I've kept it a secret. I will tell you, Prus, but you must keep it to yourself. Ellina— Ellina Makropoulos—is my aunt.

PRUS (*in astonishment*). Your aunt?

EMILIA. Yes. My mother's sister. Now you know everything.

PRUS (*ironically*). Of course, that explains it very nicely.

EMILIA. You understand?

PRUS (*getting up*). It's too bad it isn't true, Mademoiselle Marty.

EMILIA. Do you mean to say I am lying?

PRUS. I am sorry to say—yes. Had you said that she was a great-grandmother of yours, it would have been better proof.

EMILIA. Yes, you are right. (*She goes up to the throne and sits. She extends her hand to* PRUS.) Good-by.

PRUS (*Following her, he kneels in mock homage and kisses her hand*). May I express my deep admiration for you?

EMILIA. Thank you. (PRUS *starts to leave.*) Wait a moment. What would you sell that sealed envelope to me for?

PRUS (*turning round*). Pardon?

EMILIA.   I'll buy those letters. I'll give you as much as you want.

PRUS.   I beg your pardon, I cannot consider it here—and with you. Will you please send somebody else to me?

EMILIA.   Why?

PRUS.   So that I may kick him downstairs. (*With a slight bow he leaves*—EMILIA *sits without moving, her eyes closed*—GREGOR *enters. He remains standing in silence.*)

EMILIA (*after a while*).   Is it you, Berti?

GREGOR.   Why do you keep your eyes closed? You look as if you were suffering. What is the matter?

EMILIA.   I am tired. Speak softly.

GREGOR.   Softly? I warn you, if I speak softly I won't know what I am saying—I shall say foolish things. Do you hear, Emilia? I love you. I am mad. I love you—you don't laugh? I wanted you to get up and box my ears. I would have loved you the more for it. I love you. What—what is the matter?

EMILIA.   It is cold, Berti. Everyone—everything—is cold.

GREGOR.   Yes. You are cold to me but it makes me happy. Even that—I would like to strangle you when you torture me. I would like—— Ah, I am a fool, Emilia. Some day I will kill you. In you there is something awful. You are bad, low.

EMILIA.   No, Berti.

GREGOR.   Yes. Nothing means anything to you. Cruel, cold—as cold as the dead. (*Softly*) Listen—it is hell to love you. But I do. I love you so much I could tear the flesh from my body!

EMILIA.   Do you like the name Makropoulos?

GREGOR.   Stop. Don't play with me. I would give my

life if I could, for you. (*He sinks down on the bottom step of the dais.*) You can do with me whatever you want—whatever you want. I am lost, Emilia.

EMILIA.   Then listen to me. Go to your lawyer and tell him to give you the document I sent him.

GREGOR.   It is false?

EMILIA.   No, Berti. I swear on my soul it isn't. But we must have another one—with the name Makropoulos. Wait. I will explain to you. Ellian——

GREGOR.   Never mind. I've had enough of your tricks.

EMILIA.   No. Wait. You want to be rich, Berti. I want you to be rich.

GREGOR.   And will you love me?

EMILIA.   Now, stop that! Berti, you promised to get the Greek papers for me. Prus has them. Do you hear? But first you must get the inheritance.

GREGOR.   Will you love me?

EMILIA.   Never. Do you understand? Never.

GREGOR (*collapsing at her feet*).   I will kill you, Emilia.

EMILIA.   Nonsense! I could say four words to you and it would all be over. Look! Look! (*She rises.*) You'd like to kill me. Do you see the scar on my shoulder? (*She bares her shoulder.*) Another one wanted to kill me. Am I made only for your killing?

GREGOR.   I love you.

EMILIA.   Then kill yourself, you fool! But what will it come to? Your love? Oh, if you knew. If you knew how funny you are, you child. (*Her voice drops.*) If you knew how tired I am. If you knew how it's all the same to me. Oh, if you knew! (*She falls back in the throne.*)

GREGOR.   What is the matter with you?

EMILIA.   Unhappy Ellina!

GREGOR.   Come here, Emilia. We are going away. No

one ever loved you so much as I—I know—— There is
something desperate in you—something terrible, Emilia.
But I am young and strong and I can bring love to you.
Then you can forget and throw me away. Do you hear,
Emilia? (EMILIA *has fallen asleep—she breathes heavily.*
GREGOR *rises in excitement*) What is it? She's asleep. Are
you fooling? (*He stretches out his hands*) Emilia. (*He
bends over her—*THE SCRUBWOMAN *enters and coughs
warningly and severely*)

GREGOR. Who is it? Oh! The lady fell asleep. Don't
wake her. (*He kisses* EMILIA'S *hand and hurries off.*)

SCRUBWOMAN (*coming near* EMILIA *and silently looking
at her*). I am kind of sorry for her. (*Shaking her head,
she walks slowly away—*JANEK *enters from the back of the
stage. He comes down by the throne and stares at* EMILIA.)

EMILIA. Ah! Is it you, Berti?

JANEK. No, please. It is just Janek.

EMILIA (*sitting up*). Janek! Come here, Janek. Would
you like to do something for me?

JANEK. Yes, I would.

EMILIA. Anything I want you to?

JANEK. Yes.

EMILIA. Something big, Janek? An heroic deed?

JANEK. Yes.

EMILIA. And will you ask for something as a reward?

JANEK. Oh, no!

EMILIA. Come nearer. You know, you are very nice.
Listen. Your father has a sealed envelope and on it is
written, "For the hands of my son Ferdinand." It's either
in his desk or in his safe or—I don't know where.

JANEK. Yes?

EMILIA. Will you bring it to me?

JANEK. Will Father give it to me?

EMILIA.   No, he won't. You'll have to take it.

JANEK.   That isn't possible.

EMILIA.   Oh! Are you afraid of your father?

JANEK.   I'm not afraid, but——

EMILIA.   But, Janek, on my honor, it is just a remembrance—a matter of sentiment—without any value—I'd like so much to have it.

JANEK.   I—I will try.

EMILIA.   You promise? (PRUS *enters from a shadow.*)

PRUS.   You needn't trouble yourself, Janek. It is in the safe.

JANEK.   Father, again.

PRUS.   Go! (JANEK *hurries out. To* EMILIA) Purely by accident, I swear. I thought he was hanging round the theater house because of Kristina, but——

EMILIA.   And why are you hanging round the theater?

PRUS.   I was waiting—for you.

EMILIA (*stepping nearer to him*).   To give me that envelope?

PRUS.   It isn't mine to give.

EMILIA.   But—you will bring it to me? (*She comes close to him. Her lips almost touching his.*)

PRUS.   Ah! When?

EMILIA.   Tonight?

PRUS.   Tonight. (*He bows over her hand.*)

END OF ACT II

ACT III

(*The sitting room of a hotel suite. At the left is a window; and on the right is a door into the corridor. In the center is a curtained entrance into* EMILIA'S *bedroom.*

EMILIA *comes out of the bedroom in negligée, followed by* PRUS *in evening clothes, tying his tie.* PRUS, *without a word, sits down on the right.* EMILIA *goes to the window, pulls up the curtain and looks out.*)

EMILIA. A gray dawn. (*She turns back to* PRUS.) Well? (*There is a pause in which neither moves.*) Give it to me. (*There is another pause; then she speaks sharply to him.*) Do you hear? Give me that envelope. (PRUS *reaches inside his coat for a leather wallet, takes out a sealed envelope and places it on the table.* EMILIA *grabs the envelope and hurries to her dressing table. She sits down, lights a lamp, looks at the seal, hesitates, then quickly cuts it open with a hairpin and pulls out a faded yellow manuscript. With a gasp of joy she quickly folds and hides it in her bosom. She rises.*) Good!

PRUS (*after a moment's silence; quietly*). You have robbed me.

EMILIA (*with a sneer*). You had—just what you wanted.

PRUS. You have robbed me. As cold as ice. As if I were holding a corpse. (*He shudders.*) And for that, I have given you these papers that didn't belong to me. A nice business.

61

EMILIA.   Are you sorry you gave me the sealed envelope?

PRUS.   I'm sorry I met you. I should not have given it to you. Just as if I stole it! Terrible . . . terrible!

EMILIA.   Do you want some breakfast?

PRUS.   I want nothing. (*He goes over to her.*) Let me look at you. I don't know what was in the envelope. Perhaps it is of some value. But—even if it had only the value of being sealed—only the value—that I didn't know what was in it.

EMILIA.   Would you like to spit into my face?

PRUS.   No. It is myself I blame. (*Knocking is heard.*)

EMILIA (*going to the door*).   Who is it?

CHAMBERMAID (*outside*).   It is I, Madam.

EMILIA.   Come in. (*She unlocks the door. To* PRUS.) Won't you have something to eat?

CHAMBERMAID (*entering in her kimono, out of breath*). Please, Madam, isn't Baron Prus here?

PRUS (*turning round*).   Yes, what is it?

CHAMBERMAID.   One of your servants is outside. He wants to speak to you. He says it's something very important.

PRUS.   How the devil did he know I was here? Tell him to wait. No. Hold on. I'll go. (*To* EMILIA) Just a minute. (*He leaves*)

EMILIA.   Will you comb my hair? (*She sits down at the dressing table.*)

CHAMBERMAID (*letting down* EMILIA'*s hair*).   Lord! How frightened I was. The porter came running to me and said that there was a servant here and that he had to see you. He was white as a sheet, that man. He couldn't even speak. It was as if something had hit him. Something must have happened, Madam.

EMILIA (*petulantly*). Take care, you're hurting me.

CHAMBERMAID. Baron Prus is a great man, isn't he? I'd like to know what's happened. If you saw, Madam, how that servant trembled!

EMILIA (*not at all interested*). Will you have some breakfast cooked for me?

CHAMBERMAID. And he had a letter or something in his hand. Shouldn't I go and see what it is? (EMILIA *yawns.*)

EMILIA. What time is it?

CHAMBERMAID. After seven.

EMILIA. Put out the light and be quiet.

CHAMBERMAID (*She puts out the light, talking all the while*). And his lips were almost blue, the lips of that servant. I thought he was going to faint. (*She starts combing* EMILIA's *hair.*) And the tears in his eyes.

EMILIA. You're pulling my hair. You pull—give me the comb. Now look. See how much hair you've pulled out.

CHAMBERMAID. But my hands tremble so. Something must have happened.

EMILIA. I'm not going to let you pull my hair out, just because of that. Now, hurry up. (PRUS *returns from the corridor with an unopened letter in his hand.*) It didn't take you long. (PRUS *searches with his hand for a chair to sit down.*) What will you have for breakfast?

PRUS (*hoarsely*). Send—that girl——

EMILIA. Well, go then, until I ring. Go (CHAMBERMAID *goes out. After a pause*) Well, what?

PRUS (*quietly, but with great feeling*). Janek shot himself.

EMILIA (*apparently not in the least moved*). Go on.

PRUS. He's dead. His head—shattered beyond recognition.

EMILIA.   Poor boy. Who told you?

PRUS.   The servant. Janek—wrote this. They found it by his side—here, blood——

EMILIA.   What does he say?

PRUS.   I'm afraid to open it. How—how—how could he have known that I was with you? Why did he send it here? Do you think that—

EMILIA.   That he saw you?

PRUS.   Why did he do it? Why—kill himself?

EMILIA.   Read it.

PRUS.   Won't you open it? (*He gets up and steps over to her.*)

EMILIA.   No.

PRUS.   I think—that it has something to do with you —— Please open it.

EMILIA.   Oh, no.

PRUS.   You mean I must?

EMILIA.   Yes.

PRUS.   All right. (*He tears open the envelope and reads the letter.* EMILIA *goes back to her dressing table and begins to manicure her nails.*) Oh! (*He drops into a chair. The letter flutters to the floor.*)

EMILIA.   How old was he?

PRUS.   I understand. I understand.

EMILIA.   Poor Janek.

PRUS.   He loved you.

EMILIA.   Ah.

PRUS.   My only son. (*He covers his face and sobs.*) He was eighteen—only eighteen. Janek, my boy. (*Raising his arms above his head.*) God! God! I used to be too hard— too cold—I never was kind to him—I never praised him. And the boy adored me!

EMILIA.   Didn't you know that?

PRUS. Oh, God! If he were only alive. How stupid to fall in love so senselessly! He saw me come here—he waited two hours at the door—then he went home and——

EMILIA (*starting once more to comb her hair*). Poor boy.

PRUS. And only eighteen. My Janek—my child—dead —past recognition—and he wrote: "Papa, I understand. But, Papa, be happy." (*He gets up and, for the first time, notices* EMILIA.) What are you doing?

EMILIA (*with hairpins in her month*). Combing my hair.

PRUS. Perhaps you—don't understand. Janek loved you and killed himself for you.

EMILIA. Well, so many kill themselves.

PRUS. And you can comb your hair?

EMILIA. Should I run around with my hair flying, just for that?

PRUS (*striding over to her with his hand upraised to strike*). He killed himself for you! Don't you hear?

EMILIA. Well, is that my fault? Perhaps I ought to tear my hair for you, too. My maid pulls it enough.

PRUS. Stop! Or—— (*He is about to strike when there is a knock on the door.*)

EMILIA. Come in.

CHAMBERMAID (*opening the door*). Mr. Hauk-Sendorf wishes to see you, Madam.

EMILIA. Bring him in.

PRUS (*almost speechless with amazement and anger*). You—you will admit him—now—while I am here?

EMILIA. You can go in the other room for a while.

PRUS. Oh—you—you! (*He goes*—HAUK-SENDORF *enters.*)

EMILIA. *Buenos dias,* Max. Why so early?

HAUK-SENDORF. Sh-sh. (*He tiptoes over to her and kisses her on the neck.*) Dress yourself quickly, Eugenie! We are going.

EMILIA. Where?

HAUK-SENDORF. Home. To Spain. My wife doesn't know. Don't you see, I can't go back to her now. *Por Dios, Eugenie.* Make haste.

EMILIA. Are you mad?

HAUK-SENDORF. No. I am being watched. They caught me once and sent me back. Sss, like baggage, you know. Eh? I want to run away. And you will take me away?

EMILIA. To Spain? What could I do there?

HAUK-SENDORF. Ola. You could dance, of course. *Dios mio,* little girl. How jealous I used to be. You will dance. *Sabe?* And I will clap my hands. (*He takes some castanets out of his pocket.*) *Ay salero.* (*He sings.*) La, la, la. (*He stops suddenly.*) Who is crying here?

EMILIA. Oh, nobody.

HAUK-SENDORF. Sss. Someone was crying. A man's voice. Listen, *chica!*

EMILIA. Oh, yes. Somebody living next door. His son died, or something like that.

HAUK-SENDORF. Oh, I see. His son died. Oh, that is sad. Let us go, Gitana. See what I am taking along—jewels. Matilda's jewels. Matilda, my wife. Eh? She is old, you know. It is ugly to be old. It is terrible to be old. I was old once but since you came back, little one, I am only twenty years old. Eh? You don't believe?

EMILIA. *Si, si, señor.*

HAUK-SENDORF. And you don't get older. Listen. One shouldn't get old. You know, the foolish have a long life. Oh, I shall live a long time. And as long as one enjoys love—— (*He shakes the castanets.*) Enjoy love! La, la, la, la. Ssh, Gypsy, will you go?

EMILIA.   Yes.

HAUK-SENDORF.   A new life, isn't it? We will start again from twenty, little girl! You know, delight—paradise! Aha, do you remember, only just remember. All the rest is nothing. Nina, shall we go? Nina, shall we go?

EMILIA.   Yes, come along, *chu cho.* (*Someone knocks.*) Come in.

CHAMBERMAID.   Mr. Gregor wishes to see you.

HAUK-SENDORF.   What does he want here? *Dios mio.* Let's run away.

EMILIA.   Just wait. (GREGOR, KOLONATY, VITEK *and* KRISTINA *enter.*) Good morning, Berti. Who are with you, please?

GREGOR.   You're not alone?

HAUK-SENDORF.   Ah, Mr. Gregor, what a pleasure!

GREGOR (*pushing* HAUK-SENDORF *aside he brings* KRISTINA *across to* EMILIA).   Look into this child's eyes! Do you know what's happened?

EMILIA.   Janek, Janek.

GREGOR.   And do you know why?

EMILIA.   Baa!

GREGOR.   That boy is on your conscience!

EMILIA.   And is that why you are dragging people here with a lawyer?

GREGOR.   Not only for that. Don't be so impertinent, if you please.

EMILIA.   Well, will you listen to that! What do you want?

GREGOR.   You will see. What is your name, anyway?

EMILIA.   Are you cross-examining me?

KOLONATY.   Oh, no, Madam. Only a friendly chat.

GREGOR.   Let me see, Vitek. (*He takes a photograph from* VITEK.) Did you sign this photograph for Miss Kristina? Is that your signature?

EMILIA.   It is.

KOLONATY.   Very well. And now, did you send this paper to me yesterday? It is an authentic proclamation of Ellian MacGregor saying that she is the mother of Ferdinand Gregor. The date is 1836. Is that correct?

EMILIA.   It is.

KOLONATY (*triumphantly*).   But it is written with fresh ink. Do you know what that means, eh? That is a false document, my much esteemed lady!

EMILIA.   How do you know that?

GREGOR.   Look, gentlemen! (*He wets his finger and runs over the paper.*) It still smudges. What do you say to that?

EMILIA.   Nothing.

GREGOR.   It was written yesterday. Do you understand? And with the same hand that signed this photograph. A very extraordinary handwriting.

KOLONATY.   Like Greek. Upon my soul, this alpha——

GREGOR.   Did you write this paper or didn't you?

EMILIA.   I won't be cross-questioned by you.

HAUK-SENDORF.   But, gentlemen, gentlemen, permit me—— (*He comes down and makes a feeble attempt to get between them and* EMILIA.)

KOLONATY.   You keep out, Sir, keep out. These are very interesting matters, Madam. Can you tell us at least where you got this paper?

EMILIA.   I swear that Ellian MacGregor wrote it.

KOLONATY.   When? Yesterday morning?

EMILIA.   That doesn't matter.

KOLONATY. That does matter, my dear lady. That matters very much. When did Ellian MacGregor die?

EMILIA. That's enough. I shall say nothing more. (*She takes a few steps away and turns her back.*)

PRUS (*coming out of the bedroom, quickly*). Will you gentlemen show me the paper?

KOLONATY. You?

GREGOR. You have been here? Emilia, what does this mean?

HAUK-SENDORF. My, my, my! Baron Prus. What a pleasure! How are you?

KOLONATY. Do you know that your son——

PRUS (*coolly*). Yes. That paper, if you please. (KOLONATY *hands it over to him.*) Thank you.

GREGOR (*still near* EMILIA. *In a low voice*). What was he doing here? Tell me.

EMILIA. What right have you to ask?

GREGOR. The right of one who loves you.

PRUS (*laying down the paper and looking up*). That writing is genuine.

KOLONATY. Well, well. So Ellian MacGregor wrote that?

PRUS. No. The Greek, Ellina Makropoulos. It is the same handwriting that is in my letters. Unmistakably.

KOLONATY. But the signature here—is——

PRU. ——Ellina Makropoulos. There was no such person as Ellian MacGregor, gentlemen. That letter is a mistake.

KOLONATY. Upon my word! And the similarity of the photograph? (*He hands* PRUS *the photograph.*)

PRUS (*looking it over*). Unmistakably the handwriting of Ellina Makropoulos.

KOLONATY. Well, well. And it is genuine, the signature on this letter?

PRUS. Yes. Thank you. Excuse my interruption. (*He sits down at the side, with his head in his hands.*)

KOLONATY. In God's name, who understands this now?

VITEK. Perhaps it is only an accident that the handwriting of Miss Marty is somewhat similar.

KOLONATY. Of course, Vitek. And the lady's arrival is also an accident and that falsification is also only an accident. And do you know what, Vitek? You'll fill yourself up on your accidents!

EMILIA (*suddenly turning on them*). I should like to call your attention, gentlemen, to the fact that I plan to go away this morning.

GREGOR. Where to, may I ask?

EMILIA. Across the boundary.

KOLONATY. Dear lady, don't do that. You don't understand. You must stay of your own accord so that we shan't have to turn to—so that we shan't have to call in——

EMILIA. The police—— You want to have me arrested?

GREGOR. Not yet. You still have a chance. (*Knocking*)

EMILIA. Come in.

CHAMBERMAID (*sticking her head through the doorway*). Two gentlemen are looking for Mr. Hauk-Sendorf.

HAUK-SENDORF. What's that? After me? I won't go. The devil! Don't let them in——

VITEK. I will see them. (*He goes out.*)

KOLONATY (*crossing to* KRISTINA). Now, Kristina, don't cry. (*He puts his arm on her shoulder.*) I'm so sorry.

HAUK-SENDORF (*going up to* KRISTINA). My, my!

Isn't she pretty? Let's see. For the love of God, don't cry!

GREGOR (*close to* EMILIA, *in a low voice*). There is an auto below. You will ride with me across the frontier or else——

EMILIA. Ha, ha. Is that what you counted on?

GREGOR. I, or the police? Are you going?

EMILIA. No.

VITEK (*re-entering*). It is a physician and another gentleman, waiting for Mr. Hauk-Sendorf. They are supposed to take him home.

HAUK-SENDORF (*to* EMILIA). So you see. Ho, ho. They have me already. (*To* VITEK.) Won't you ask them to wait?

VITEK. I told them to.

GREGOR. Gentlemen, since Mademoiselle Marty doesn't intend to explain, we will be so bold as to look through her trunks and papers.

KRISTINA. No, you haven't the right, Gregor.

GREGOR (*to* KOLONATY). Shall we call the police, then?

KOLONATY. I wash my hands of the affair.

HAUK-SENDORF. Permit me, Mr. Gregor, as a gentleman——

GREGOR. Behind the door your physician and the other man are waiting. Shall I invite them in?

HAUK-SENDORF. Oh, not that, please. But, Baron Prus, certainly——

PRUS. Do—with that woman—whatever you want to.

GREGOR. All right, let's start. (*He goes to her desk*)

EMILIA. Let it alone! (*She opens the drawer of her dresser.*) If you dare!

KOLONATY (*jumping to her and catching her arm*). Oh, Madam! (*He pulls a revolver out of her hand. She sinks into a chair.*)

GREGOR (*at the desk, without turning*). What is it? She wanted to shoot?

KOLONATY. Yes, it's loaded. Gregor, let's leave this alone. Let me call someone in?

GREGOR. We can fix it up ourselves.

EMILIA (*to* HAUK-SENDORF). Max, will you permit it? And you are a gentleman!

HAUK-SENDORF. *Cielo de mi.* What am I to do?

EMILIA (*to* HAUK-SENDORF). Baa, you are old. (*To* PRUS.) Baron Prus, you are a gentleman, at least. You cannot permit——

PRUS. I ask you not to speak to me.

KRISTINA (*sobbing*). It is terrible, what you are doing to her. Let her alone.

KOLONATY. That is what I say, too, Kristina. What we are doing is unfair—cruel.

GREGOR (*throwing out a bunch of papers on the table*). There, Madam. You're carrying a whole archive with you. (*He goes into the bedroom.*)

KOLONATY (*picking up one or two of the papers*). That's something for you, Vitek. The daintiest papers. Don't you want to sort them?

EMILIA. Don't you dare to read them!

KOLONATY. Oh, dear Madam, I beg of you not to move. Otherwise I should have to threaten you with bodily harm and injury. Paragraph ninety-one of the criminal code.

EMILIA. And you are a lawyer.

KOLONATY. You see, I have acquired a taste for crime. I think that I always had a talent for it. Sometimes one doesn't recognize one's real abilities until old age. I want you to know I am a sort of Arsene Lupin.

VITEK. Permit me, Mademoiselle Marty. Where are **you** going to sing next? (*He receives no answer*)

HAUK-SENDORF. *Mon dieu, je suis desolé—desolé.*

VITEK. And did you read the criticisms about yourself?

EMILIA. No.

VITEK (*taking some clippings out of his pocket*). They are marvelous, Madam. For example, "A voice of extraordinary brilliance and power. Overpowering fullness of high tones. Serene certainty in singing," and so on. "The wonderful appearance evoked—incomparable dramatic interpretation. An achievement unique in the history of opera, and perhaps of operatic art as a whole in history." Madam, imagine! (*No one is listening to him, so he stops and begins to sort the papers.*)

GREGOR (*returning from the bedroom with an armful of papers*). There, Doctor, we have enough for a while. (*He throws the papers on the table.*)

KOLONATY. With pleasure. (*He smells the papers.*) They are full of dust, Madam. Vitek, the dust is historical.

GREGOR. I found a seal with the initials E. M. The same seal that is on the paper of Ellian MacGregor.

PRUS (*standing up*). Let me see.

KOLONATY (*examining the papers*). The devil, Vitek, here is the date, sixteen hundred and three!

PRUS (*reading the seal*). It is the seal of Ellina Makropoulos. (*He sits down.*)

KOLONATY. So, you see what one finds.

HAUK-SENDORF. But good Lord!

GREGOR. Mr. Hauk-Sendorf, don't you know this medallion? I think that your coat of arms is on it.

HAUK-SENDORF (*looking at the medallion*). Yes—it is —I gave it to her, myself.

GREGOR. When?

HAUK-SENDORF. Well—in Spain—fifty years ago.

GREGOR. To whom?

HAUK-SENDORF. To herself—to Eugenie—Eugenie Montez.

KOLONATY (*looking up from the papers*). Here is something Spanish. Do you know Spanish?

HAUK-SENDORF. Oh, yes. Let me see. He, he! Eugenie, this is from Madrid.

KOLONATY. What?

HAUK-SENDORF. From the police. Banishment—Ramera Gitana, who is called Eugenie Montez. Ha, ha, ha! I know! Because of that fight, wasn't it?

KOLONATY. I beg your pardon. (*He bows to* EMILIA; *then continues his examination of the papers.*) A passport. Elsa Muller, seventy-nine. Death certificate—of Ellian MacGregor, eighteen thirty-six. Look! Look! All jumbled up! Just wait, Madam, we will get to your own name. Ekaterina Myskin. Now, who is that?

VITEK. Ekaterina Myskin was a Russian singer in the forties.

KOLONATY. You know everything, man.

GREGOR. That's extraordinary. All the initials are E. M.

KOLONATY. Apparently, Madam collects only those initials. A special hobby, isn't it? Hello, what is this? "Dein Pepi." (*He steps over to* PRUS.) That is apparently your great-grand-uncle, Prus. Shall I read it to you? "Meine liebste, liebste Ellian."

PRUS. Emilia, isn't it?

KOLONATY. Oh, no. Ellian, and on the envelope, "Ellian MacGregor, Royal Opera House, Vienna." Wait, Gregor. We will still win on Ellian. "Meine liebste, liebste Ellian."

EMILIA. Stop. Don't read any more. Those are my papers.

KOLONATY. But they are very interesting to us.

EMILIA. Don't read them. (*Stepping forward.*) I shall tell everything myself. Everything you ask me.

KOLONATY. Really?

EMILIA. I swear.

KOLONATY (*folding the papers*). Then we beg your pardon a million times—that we had to force you this way.

EMILIA. Are you going to pass judgment on me?

KOLONATY. No, no. It will be just a friendly chat.

EMILIA. But I want you to judge me. It must be like the inquisition.

KOLONATY. But——

EMILIA. Please, it is my wish.

HAUK-SENDORF. Ssh—the inquisition—Spain—He, he!

KOLONATY. Aha, I see. (*To* EMILIA) Very well, we will convene an inquisitorial court—Vitek, lend a hand—we must arrange the courtroom. (KOLONATY *and* VITEK *quickly arrange the furniture in such a way as to suggest a courtroom. The others catch the idea and assist. The sofa is pushed back slightly to the center of the room, for the jury. A large table is placed right, for* KOLONATY *as presiding judge and inquisitor, and* VITEK *as the clerk.* EMILIA *is to sit alone at the left. While they are doing this,* HAUK-SENDORF *stands aloof and* EMILIA *goes to her dressing table and, picking up a bottle and glass, takes a long drink. The court is by this time arranged and they all turn towards* EMILIA.)

KOLONATY. Take it away.

EMILIA (*holding* VITEK *off*). No, or I won't speak. (*She pours out another glass.*) This is only for courage. (*She drinks.*)

KOLONATY. The court will sit. (*All take their places except* EMILIA, *who stands in a defiant attitude by her dressing table.* KOLONATY, *pointing to her chair, speaks sharply.*) Your place is there. Sit down. (EMILIA *drops into the chair.*) Gregor, I appoint you public prosecutor. Recite the accusation.

GREGOR (*rising*).   The accused, Emilia Marty, a singer. She is accused before God and us of fraud and falsification of papers for her own selfish purposes. And furthermore and in addition, she has transgressed against all trust and decency—against life itself! That does not belong to human judgment. She will have to answer for that in a higher court. (*He sits down.*)

KOLONATY.   Has anybody anything to say for the accused? No one? Then we may proceed with the cross-examination. (*He rises.*) Stand up, accused. What is your name?

EMILIA (*standing up*).   I?

KOLONATY.   Of course. You! You! You! What is your name?

EMILIA (*calmly*).   Ellina Makropoulos.

KOLONATY (*excitedly*).   What?

EMILIA   Ellina Makropoulos.

KOLONATY.   Born where?

EMILIA.   In Crete.

KOLONATY.   When?

EMILIA.   When?

KOLONATY.   How old are you?

EMILIA.   Well, how old do you think?

KOLONATY.   I should say about thirty.

VITEK.   Over thirty.

KRISTINA.   Over forty.

EMILIA (*sticks out her tongue at* KRISTINA).   Toad!

KOLONATY.   Behave! You must respect your judges.

EMILIA.   Do I look that old?

KOLONATY. When were you born?

EMILIA. Fifteen hundred and eighty-five.

KOLONATY. What?

EMILIA. Fifteen hundred and eighty-five.

KOLONATY. In the year eighty-five. Then you are thirty-nine years old, aren't you?

EMILIA. Three hundred and thirty-nine years, if you please.

KOLONATY. I ask you once more to speak seriously. How old are you?

EMILIA. Three hundred and thirty-nine years.

KOLONATY. Well, upon my word! And who was your father?

EMILIA. Hieronymus Makropoulos, the personal physician of Emperor Rudolph II.

KOLONATY (*completely exasperated*). To hell with you! I'm not going to talk to her! (*He sits down and* PRUS *rises.*)

PRUS. What is your real name?

EMILIA. Ellina Makropoulos.

PRUS. What! Ellina Makropoulos, the mistress of Joseph Prus?

EMILIA (*with a little bow*). You put it nicely.

PRUS. What?

EMILIA (*with a gay bravado*). Yes, I was the mistress of Pepi Prus. Gregor's our son.

GREGOR. And Ellian MacGregor?

EMILIA. That is I.

GREGOR. Are you raving?

EMILIA. I am your great-grandmother, or something like that. Ferdi was my boy. Do you understand?

GREGOR. Which Ferdi?

EMILIA. Ferdinand Gregor, but he is in the birth-record as Ferdinand Makropoulos because—well, there I gave his real name.

KOLONATY. And when were you born?

EMILIA (*raising her arms*). Fifteen hundred and eighty-five. *Christos Soter!* Leave me in peace.

HAUK-SENDORF. And—and excuse me, but you are Eugenie Montez?

EMILIA. I was, Max; I was. But then I was only two hundred and ninety years old; and I was also Ekatorina Myskina, and Elsa Muller and all the others. (*Turning to the others*) One cannot live with you more than thirty years at a time.

KOLONATY. Especially not a singer.

EMILIA. I should think not!

VITEK. And you lived, if I may ask, in the eighteenth century?

EMILIA. Of course.

VITEK. You knew—Danton personally?

EMILIA. I knew him. He was a disgusting man.

PRUS. And how did you know what was in Pepi's will?

EMILIA. Because Pepi told me before he put it there so I could tell that stupid fool—Ferdi Gregor.

GREGOR. Why didn't you tell him?

EMILIA (*with a shrug of the shoulders*). Oh, I simply cannot be bothered with my brats.

HAUK-SENDORF. My, my, my, how you talk!

EMILIA. My dear, it is a long time since I was a lady.

VITEK. Did you have any more children?

EMILIA. About twenty, I think. One loses count. (*Picking up the bottle and glass.*) Wouldn't someone else like to drink? Ah, the dryness in my mouth. I'll burn. (*She drinks and falls back in the chair.*)

PRUS. There are letters here signed E. M. Were those written by you?

EMILIA. They were; you know it. Give them back to me. I like to read them sometimes. Beastly, isn't it?

PRUS. Did you write them as Ellina Makropoulos or Ellian MacGregor?

EMILIA. It is all the same. Pepi knew who I was. I told him everything. I liked him.

HAUK-SENDORF (*getting up in excitement*). Eugenie!

EMILIA. Keep quiet, Max. I liked you, too. It was nice to live with you, when you were a young ensign. But Pepi—(*Her voice breaks.*)—I liked him the best of all. That is why I lent him—the Makropoulos secret—when he wanted it so much——

PRUS. What did you lend him?

EMILIA. The Makropoulos secret.

PRUS. What is that?

EMILIA. That paper you gave me back today. The sealed envelope. Pepi wanted to try it. He promised to give it back—but instead of that he hid it with the will. Perhaps, so that I would have to come and get it—but I didn't come until now. (*She laughs, then suddenly stops and turns to* PRUS.) How did Pepi die?

PRUS. In fever and with terrible cramps.

EMILIA. That was it! That was it! *Aia Maria!* I told him so!

GREGOR. And you came here just for that Greek thing?

EMILIA. Ha, ha! I'm not going to give it to you. No, my dear fellow. And you thought, Berti, that I came just to help you and your silly case! I don't care a damn if you win. All I want is that secret.

GREGOR. Why?

EMILIA. Because I'm getting old. Because I'm at the

end. I want to try it again. Feel, Berti, how icy I am getting. Feel my hands. Ah, God! My hands!

HAUK-SENDORF.   What is the Makropoulos secret, if you please?

EMILIA.   It is written there how one does it.

HAUK-SENDORF.   How one does what?

EMILIA.   How a human being can live for three hundred years. To be young for three hundred years. My father wrote that for Emperor Rudolph. You don't know anything about it, do you?

VITEK.   Only from history.

EMILIA.   You can't tell anything from history. That's nonsense! *Penaia—* What did I want to say? (*She takes a pinch of something out of a snuff box.*) Does anybody want some?

GREGOR.   What is that?

EMILIA.   Nothing, nothing. What was I talking about?

VITEK.   About Emperor Rudolph.

EMILIA.   Aha, he was an immoral man! Just wait! I could tell you things about him!

KOLONATY.   The court is not interested.

EMILIA.   Well, anyway, when he started to grow old —he kept looking about for an elixir of life, or something, to make him young again, you see. Then my father came to him and wrote that—that thing—so he could stay young for three hundred years. But Emperor Rudolph was afraid it was poison and wanted to try it first on the doctor's daughter. That was I. I was sixteen then. So Father tried it on me. He called it a "charm," but it belonged to the devil.

HAUK-SENDORF.   What was it?

EMILIA.   I must not say. I lay for a week or longer, beside myself in fever. But I got well.

VITEK. And the Emperor?

EMILIA. Did nothing. He went mad. How could he be sure that I was going to live for three hundred years? So he put my father in a tower as a fraud and I ran away with everything he had written to Hungary or to Turkey, I don't remember which.

KOLONATY. Did you show the charm to anyone—the Makropoulos secret?

EMILIA. I did. A Tyrolian priest tried it in sixteen-sixty, or thereabouts. Perhaps he is still alive, I don't know. At one time he was Pope and called himself Alexander, or Pius, or something like that. Then a Statia officer—but he was killed. Ugo was his name. Heavens! What a good-looking man he was! Then at Nageli there was Andrew, and a good-for-nothing Bombita and Pepi Prus, who died of it. Pepi was the last one—and it remained with him. And now I don't know any more. Ask Bombita. Bombita is alive, but I don't know what his name is now.

KOLONATY (*rising and taking her by the shoulders*). Pardon me, but you are now two hundred and forty-nine years old, aren't you?

EMILIA. No, three hundred and thirty-nine.

KOLONATY. You are intoxicated. From the year fifteen eighty-five to the present day is two hundred and forty-nine years, isn't it?

EMILIA. My God! Don't try to confuse me! Three hundred and thirty-nine.

KOLONATY. Why did you forge the handwriting of Ellian MacGregor?

EMILIA. Why? I, myself, am Ellian MacGregor!

KOLONATY. Do not lie! You are Emilia Marty.

EMILIA. Yes, but only for the last twelve years.

KOLONATY.   Then do you confess that you stole the medallion of Eugenie Montez—Eh?

EMILIA.   Good Lord! That is not true. Eugenie Montez——

KOLONATY.   It is in the accusation. You acknowledged it.

EMILIA.   That is not true!

KOLONATY.   Who is your accomplice?

EMILIA.   There isn't one.

KOLONATY.   Do not deny it. We know everything. When were you born?

EMILIA (*weakly*).   Fifteen eighty-five.

KOLONATY (*He produces a glass filled with some liquid*). Drink a full glass of this.

EMILIA.   No, I don't want to! Leave me alone!

KOLONATY.   You must! A full glass, quick! (*He puts it to her lips.*)

EMILIA (*in terror*).   What are you doing to me? Berti! (*She drinks.*) Ah—this is—turning my—head.

KOLONATY.   What is your name?

EMILIA.   I don't feel well. (*She sinks to her knees.*)

KOLONATY (*catching her and bending back her head*). What is your name?

EMILIA.   Ellina—Makro——

KOLONATY.   Do not lie! Do you know who I am? I am a priest. Confess to me!

EMILIA.   Pater—hemon—hos—eis—en uranois—

KOLONATY.   What is your name?

EMILIA.   Ellina————poulos.

KOLONATY.   May God receive the soul of this, thine unworthy servant, Emilia Marty, m-m-m—, Amen. (*She screams.*) Stand up! Who are you?

EMILIA (*falling to the floor in a faint*).   Ellina——

KOLONATY.   Damn!

GREGOR. What is it?

KOLONATY. She isn't lying! Quick! (*He rings the bell.*) A doctor, Gregor!

KRISTINA. You've poisoned her!

KOLONATY. Slightly.

GREGOR (*at the door into the hall*). Is the doctor there, please?

PHYSICIAN (*entering*). Mr. Hauk, we have been waiting for you for an hour. Come along, now!

KOLONATY. Hold on! This first, doctor. (*Pointing to* EMILIA.)

PHYSICIAN (*kneeling beside* EMILIA). Fainted?

KOLONATY. Poisoned.

PHYSICIAN. With what? (*Leaning over* EMILIA *and smelling her mouth.*) Aha! (*He stands up.*) Put her to bed, somewhere.

KOLONATY. Gregor, carry her into the bedroom! As her closest kin——

PHYSICIAN. Is there any warm water?

PRUS. Yes. (*He rings.*)

PHYSICIAN. Fine. If you please. (*He writes a prescription.*) Black coffee—and to the pharmacy with this. (*He goes into the bedroom.*)

KOLONATY. Well, then, gentlemen—— (*The* CHAMBERMAID *enters.*)

CHAMBERMAID. Did Madam ring?

KOLONATY. Yes. She would like some black coffee—very strong black coffee.

CHAMBERMAID. He, he! How do you know, Sir?——

KOLONATY. And run over to the druggist's with this. Be off! Hurry! (*The* CHAMBERMAID *goes out.*) (*Sitting down in the middle of the room.*) There's something in what she says.

PRUS. I know it.

HAUK-SENDORF. I—I—please don't laugh; but I believe her, absolutely.

KOLONATY. You, too, Prus?

PRUS. Absolutely.

KOLONATY. I do, also. Do you know what it means?

PRUS. That Gregor will get Loukov.

KOLONATY. Hm, is that very unpleasant?

PRUS. I have no heirs. (GREGOR *returns with his hand done up in a handkerchief.*)

HAUK-SENDORF. How is she?

GREGOR. A little better. But she bit me, the animal. Do you know, I believe her?

KOLONATY. We, too, alas! (*A pause.*)

HAUK-SENDORF. Good God! Three hundred years! Three—hundred—years!

KRISTINA (*shuddering*). Three hundred years. That's terrible. (*The* CHAMBERMAID *enters with coffee.*)

KOLONATY. Take it to her, Kristina. See what you can do for her. (KRISTINA *goes into her bedroom with the coffee; the* CHAMBERMAID *goes out. Making sure that both doors are closed.*) There! Now, gentlemen, what shall we do with it?

GREGOR. With what?

KOLONATY. With the Makropoulos secret. Somewhere here is a formula for a three-hundred-year life. Can we get hold of it?

PRUS. She has it in her bosom.

KOLONATY. Good! Gentlemen, it is a thing of unimaginable importance. What shall we do with it?

GREGOR. Nothing at all. The formula belongs to me. I am her heir.

KOLONATY. Keep your mouth shut! As long as she is

alive, you are not her heir; and she can live for another three hundred years, if she wants to. Don't you see, we must get hold of it.

GREGOR.   By trickery?

KOLONATY.   Why not? This is something of such importance—for us and for everybody, that—hm. Gentlemen, you understand me? Ought we to let her keep it? What? Should she alone or, at best, some such good-for-nothing as Bombita have the advantage of it? Who will get it?

GREGOR.   First of all, we must help her.

KOLONATY.   Don't worry about her. Prus, if you, yourself, had the secret in your hands, would you give it to me? You know—so I could live for three hundred years?

PRUS.   No.

KOLONATY.   You see, gentlemen, we shall have to come to some agreement among ourselves. What shall we do with it?

VITEK (*standing up and coming to the center of the group*).   We'll make the Makropoulos secret public.

KOLONATY.   Oh, no! Not that!

VITEK.   We'll give it to everybody! We'll give it to the people. Everyone—everyone has the same right to life. We live for such a short time. How insignificant! God! How insignificant it is to be a human being.

KOLONATY.   Rubbish!

VITEK.   No, gentlemen, it does mean something! Just consider—the human soul, brains, work, love—everything. Good God, what can a man do in sixty years! What does he enjoy? What does he learn? He doesn't even enjoy the fruit of the tree he has planted; he doesn't learn all that his predecessors knew; he doesn't finish his work; he dies, and he hasn't lived. Ah, God, but we live so insignificantly!

KOLONATY.   Well, Vitek——

VITEK. And he hasn't had time for gladness, and he hasn't had time to think, and he hasn't had time for anything except a desire for bread. He hasn't done anything, and he hasn't known anything. No, not even himself. Why have you lived? Has it been worth the trouble?

KOLONATY. Do you want to make me cry?

VITEK. We die like animals. What else is immortality of the soul but a protest against the shortness of life? A human being is something more than a turtle or a raven; a man needs more time to live. Sixty years—it's not right. It's weakness, it's ignorance, and it's animal-like.

HAUK-SENDORF. Oh, my, and I am already seventy-six!

VITEK. Let's give everyone a three-hundred-year life. It will be the biggest event since the creation of man; it will be the liberating and creating anew of man! God, what man will be able to do in three hundred years! To be a child and pupil for fifty years; fifty years to understand the world and its ways, and to see everything there is; and a hundred years to work in; and then a hundred years, when we have understood everything, to live in wisdom, to teach, and to give example. How valuable human life would be if it lasted for three hundred years! There would be no wars. There would be no fear, no selfishness. Everyone would be wise and dignified. (*Wringing his hands.*) Give people life! Give them full human life!

KOLONATY. Yes, that is all very nice. Very nice, but—

GREGOR. Many thanks! To be a clerk for three hundred years—or to knit socks!

VITEK. But——

GREGOR. Or to know everything. And, besides—— Why, most people are willing to live as they do only because they are ignorant.

KOLONATY. Vitek, it's absurd. Our social system is

founded on shortness of life. Take—contracts, mortgages, debts and all. No one will make a contract for three hundred years! And marriage—Why, nobody is going to stay married for three hundred years! Man, you're on anarchist. You want to revise the entire social system.

HAUK-SENDORF. And—pardon—then after three hundred years each could make himself young again—

KOLONATY. —And live forever. (*To* VITEK) Don't you see?

VITEK. Yes, but it could be forbidden. At the end of three hundred years, everyone would have to die!

KOLONATY. Will you listen to him! Now he wants to forbid people living!

HAUK-SENDORF (*to* KOLONATY). Pardon me, but I—I think that the secret could be distributed for a stipulation.

KOLONATY. How's that?

HAUK-SENDORF. Well, I mean by years, for a certain sum—ten years of life. Three hundred years is quite long and someone might not want it. But everyone would buy ten years, wouldn't they?

KOLONATY. We could establish a wholesale commerce in "years." A good idea! I can see the orders now: "Send us by mail twelve hundred years of life (prepared for people), Kohn & Co." "Express two million years, class A, well wrapped up. Viden Brothers." Hauk, that's not bad at all. (*He pats* HAUK-SENDORF *good-naturedly on the back.*)

HAUK-SENDORF. Pardon, but I—I am no merchant, see? But when a person is old, he would like—a little life —but three hundred years is too much, isn't it?

CHAMBERMAID (*entering*). If you please, here is the prescription from the drug store.

KOLONATY. Thank you. How long would you like to live?

CHAMBERMAID. Hihi, about thirty years more.

KOLONATY. No longer than that?

CHAMBERMAID. No. What would I do then? (*She laughs and looks up at* KOLONATY.)

KOLONATY. You see, Vitek. (*The* CHAMBERMAID *goes out.* KOLONATY *knocks on bedroom door.*)

PHYSICIAN (*in the doorway*). What is it? (KOLONATY *hands him the medicine.*) Ah, very good.

HAUK-SENDORF. How is the lady, please?

PHYSICIAN. Not at all well. (*He goes into bedroom.*)

PRUS (*standing up*). Gentlemen, chance has placed in our hands a certain secret. It concerns the prolonging of life. Let us admit that it is a possibility. No one of us, I hope, will abuse this knowledge.

VITEK. That's just what I say! We must prolong the life of all.

PRUS. No, only the life of the strong. The life of the most talented. For the common herd this short life is good enough.

VITEK. Oh, no!

PRUS. Please, I do not want to argue. The ordinary, small, stupid one surely does not die. He is everlasting. Littleness multiplies without ceasing, like flies and mice. Only greatness dies. Only strength and talent die—and cannot be replaced. We ought to keep it in our own hands. We can prolong the life of the aristocracy.

VITEK. Aristocracy! Do you hear that? Privilege on life!

PRUS. Only the best are important in life. Only the chief, fertile and executive men. I am not mentioning women, but there are in this world about ten or twenty, perhaps a thousand, men who are irreplaceable. We can keep them. We can develop in them superhuman reason and supernatural power. We can breed ten, a hundred or a thousand supermen—masters and creators. So, I say, select those who have the right to unlimited life.

KOLONATY. Pray tell, who would name the chosen ones? The governments? The Plebiscite? Swedish Academy?

PRUS. No idiotic voting! The strongest would hand over life to the strongest. It would be—a dynasty of the strong.

VITEK. Until the time when the rabble would claim its own right to life.

PRUS. Time would kill them off. Progress in the world would replace the small and weak despot with the strong and big despot. Privileged long life—that's the despotism of the select. That is the rule of reason. Superhuman authority in knowledge and executive ability. You have it in your hands, gentlemen. You can abuse it. I've told you all. (*He sits down.*)

KOLONATY. Hm! Do I belong to this best dozen class, or does Gregor?

PRUS. No.

GREGOR. But you do, of course.

PRUS. Not any more—not now.

GREGOR. Gentlemen, let's stop this useless talk. The Makropoulos secret belongs to the Makropoulos family. Let them do with it what they will.

VITEK. What's that you say?

GREGOR. Only the members of the family enjoy the privilege of the secret. Only he who is the descendant of Ellina Makropoulos, whoever he may be.

KOLONATY.   And he will live forever, just because he was born of some loafer or baron and a raving, hysterical woman?

GREGOR.   All the same, it will still belong to him.

KOLONATY.   This is a pretty business.

PHYSICIAN (*coming out of the bedroom*).   She is resting. Let her sleep.

HAUK-SENDORF.   Yes, yes, let her stay. That's good.

PHYSICIAN.   Come along home, Mr. Hauk-Sendorf. I'll take you.

HAUK-SENDORF.   But we're having an important conference, aren't we? Please let me stay a little longer. I——

PHYSICIAN (*taking him by the arm*).   Now, now. Someone is waiting for you outside the door. No fooling, old fellow, or——

HAUK-SENDORF.   Yes, yes—I—I—I'll come right away.

PHYSICIAN.   Your servant, gentlemen. (*He goes out.*)

KOLONATY.   Gregor, did you mean what you just said?

GREGOR.   I did.

KRISTINA (*coming out of bedroom*).   Talk quietly. She ought to sleep.

KOLONATY.   Kristina, come here. Would you like to live for three hundred years?

KRISTINA.   No.

KOLONATY.   And if you had the secret for such a long life, what would you do with it?

KRISTINA.   I don't know.

VITEK.   You'd give it to all the world, wouldn't you?

KRISTINA.   No—I don't think so. Do not ask me.

HAUK-SENDORF.   Oh, yes you would, Miss, one likes so much to live.

KRISTINA (*covering up her eyes*).   When everything

is gone? Oh, no, no! (*She crosses over to a chair and sits down.*)

PRUS (*going over to her*).   Thank you, for Janek.

KRISTINA.   Why?

PRUS.   For having thought of him now.

KRISTINA.   Thought of him? As if I could really think —of anything else.

KOLONATY.   And here we are, arguing over eternal life.

EMILIA (*coming out of the bedroom like a shadow. Everyone stands up*).   Pardon me—for having left you.

GREGOR.   How are you feeling?

EMILIA.   My head aches—desolately—abominably.

HAUK-SENDORF.   That will go away.

EMILIA.   No, it never will go away. I've had it for two hundred years.

KOLONATY.   What?

EMILIA.   Ennui. No, it isn't that. It's—oh, you people have no name for it. There's no name for it in any tongue. Bombita used to talk about it, too—it's terrible.

GREGOR.   What is it?

EMILIA.   I don't know. Everything is so dull, empty and ordinary—— Are you all here? It seems as if you were not—as if you were things or shadows. What do you want me to do?

KOLONATY.   Perhaps we ought to go?

EMILIA.   No, it doesn't matter. It's all the same, whether you're here or not. And you make such a fuss over each little death. You are queer——

VITEK.   What is the matter with you?

EMILIA (*crying out*).   One ought not, ought not, ought not to live so long!

VITEK.   Why?

EMILIA.   One can't go through with it. One lives for a hundred, or a hundred and thirty years, and then—then one realizes—then one finds out—then one's soul dies.

VITEK.   One realizes what?

EMILIA.   God! There is no word for it. Then one doesn't believe in anything. Not in anything! And from it comes that ennui. Berti, you used to say that I sang as if I were frozen. You see, art has meaning only so long as one doesn't understand; but when one understands all—one sees that singing is the same as keeping silent. Everything is the same. There is no difference in anything.

VITEK.   That's not true. When you sing—then people are moved to something better and higher.

EMILIA.   People are never better. Nothing can ever change. Nothing matters. If there were an explosion now, or an earthquake, if the end of the world were here, nothing would matter. Even I do not matter. You are here and I am far away—away from everything—— Three hundred years—oh, God, if you only knew how easy it is for you to live!

KOLONATY.   Why?

EMILIA.   You are so near to everything. For you, everything has a meaning, for you everything has some feeling. Oh, God, if I could only once more——(*She wrings her hands.*) Fools, you are so fortunate. Everything interests you—like monkeys. You believe everything; you believe in love, in yourselves, in progress, in humanity—I don't know in what. You believe in pleasure, Max. Kristina, you believe in love and faithfulness. You believe in foolishness, Vitek. Everyone, everyone believes in everything. You—fools!

VITEK.   But, why, there are—higher values—ideals—

EMILIA. Yes, but only for you. How shall I tell you? Love there may be, but it is only in you. As soon as it is not, then there is no love—nowhere in the universe. And one cannot love for three hundred years. It does not last. Everything is irksome. It is tiresome to be bad and tiresome to be good. Heaven and earth tire one. And then you find out that there truly is none. Nothing exists—neither sin, nor pain, nor desire—absolutely nothing. Only that exists which has some feeling. And for you, everything has feeling. Oh, God, I was like you once. I was a girl; I had faith; I was happy. God in heaven!

HAUK-SENDORF. What? What's happened to you?

EMILIA. If you could only understand what Bombita said to me! We old ones know altogether too much. But you have more than we, you fools! Infinitely more! You have everything. Why, you couldn't wish for anything more. You live, but in us life has stopped. And it cannot go on! God, what loneliness!

PRUS. Why did you come here—for the Makropoulos secret? Why do you want to live longer?

EMILIA (*quietly, almost in a whisper*). Because I am afraid to die.

PRUS. So even an immortal isn't spared that?

EMILIA. No. (*A pause.*)

PRUS. We have been too severe with you.

EMILIA. No, you were right. It is horrible to be so old. Do you know, children are afraid of me? Kristina, you loathe me, don't you?

KRISTINA. No! I am very sorry for you.

EMILIA. Sorry? You don't even envy me? (*A pause. She shudders and takes the folded paper from her bosom.*) Here it is written, "Ego, Hieronymus Makropoulos, iatros

Kaisoros Rudolfo—" And further on, word for word, what to do. (*She stands up*) Take it, Berti, I don't want it any more.

GREGOR.   Thank you, I don't want it, either.

EMILIA.   No? Then you, Max. You like to live. You will be able to love, see? Take it.

HAUK-SENDORF.   Please—can one die of it? And does it hurt to take it?

EMILIA.   Yes, it hurts. Are you afraid?

HAUK-SENDORF.   Yes.

EMILIA.   But you will live for three hundred years.

HAUK-SENDORF.   If—if it didn't hurt—Hihi, I don't want it.

EMILIA.   Doctor, you are a crafty man. Do you want it?

KOLONATY.   You are very kind, but I won't have anything to do with it.

EMILIA.   You are so ridiculous; Vitek, I'll give it to you. You'll probably benefit all humanity with it.

VITEK.   No, please. I think I'd—rather not.

EMILIA.   Prus, you are such a strong man. Are you, too, afraid to live for three hundred years?

PRUS.   Yes.

EMILIA.   God, then no one wants it? Are you here, Kristina? You haven't said a word. Poor girl, I took your sweetheart from you. You take it. You are beautiful; you'll live for three hundred years. You'll sing like Emilia Marty. You'll be famous. Remember, in a few years you'll begin to grow old, and then you'll repent—take it, girl!

KRISTINA (*taking the paper*).   Thank you.

VITEK.   What are you going to do with it, Krista?

KRISTINA (*opening the envelope*).   I don't know.

GREGOR.   Are you going to try it?

KOLONATY.   Isn't she afraid?—Give it back!

VITEK. Return it!

EMILIA. Leave her alone. (*The others draw back from* KRISTINA. *She silently places the paper over the burning candle.*)

VITEK. Don't burn it! It's an historical document.

KOLONATY. Wait! Don't!

HAUK-SENDORF. Good God!

GREGOR. Take it away from her.

PRUS. Leave her alone! (*They are again crushed in silence.*)

HAUK-SENDORF. Why, look, it doesn't want to burn.

GREGOR. It's parchment.

KOLONATY. How slowly it glows. Kristina, don't burn yourself.

HAUK-SENDORF. Won't you please let me have just a little bit! Just a little piece of it? (*There is a moment of silence as the paper burns.*)

VITEK. Eternal life! Humanity will search for it always, and here—here——

KOLONATY. And we might have lived forever. Nice work!

PRUS (*crossing over and putting his hand on* KOLONATY'S *shoulder*). Eternal life.—Have you any children?

KOLONATY. I have.

PRUS. So, you see, eternal life! If we only thought of birth—rather than of death. Life is not short, as long as we can be the cause of life—— (*There is a second or two of silence as the thought penetrates their minds.*)

GREGOR. It's done! Well, it was only—a wild thought, this living forever. I feel depressed and a little more at ease because it isn't possible any longer——

KOLONATY. We are no longer young. Only youth could have burned it—our fear of death. Well done, Kristina.

HAUK-SENDORF. Pardon me, but the room smells so queerly—of burnt matter—— (VITEK *opens the window and* KRISTINA *throws the ashes out.*)

EMILIA. The end of immortality! Ha, ha, ha! (*She laughs hysterically, breaking off sharply in the middle. Then quietly she raises her arms in a welcoming gesture as though to embrace Death.*)

CURTAIN